Mad About Cheddar

Mad About Cheddar

Angela Clubb

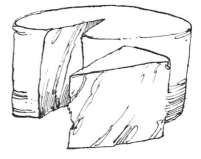

Clarke Irwin
Toronto   Canada

Copyright © 1983 Angela Clubb

Canadian Cataloguing in Publication Data

Clubb, Angela, 1949-
  Mad about cheddar

Includes index.
ISBN 0-7720-1436-1

1. Cookery (Cheese). 2. Cheddar cheese. I. Title.

TX759.C48 1983   641.6'7354   C83-099163-8

The cover photograph is reproduced with the kind permission of
The Dairy Bureau of Canada.

Typeset by ART-U Graphics
Printed in Canada by the Alger Press Limited

1 2 3 4 5 6 7 8 AP 90 89 88 87 86 85 84 83

Published by Clarke Irwin (1983) Inc.
4386 Sheppard Avenue East
Agincourt, Ontario
M1S 3B6

Contents

Introduction

Who doesn't love Cheddar?

It has long been a favourite in sandwiches, snacks and cheese platters, but its firm texture and range of flavours create endless cooking possibilities. Cheddar is wonderful in soups, casseroles, quiches and desserts. *Mad About Cheddar* includes traditional recipes as well as new, interesting ideas — all easy to prepare.

A whole food, rich in protein and vitamins, Cheddar is an ideal meat substitute. Teamed with vegetables or pasta, a little Cheddar goes a long way to become a satisfying meal.

Canadian Cheddar has a distinct flavour that the British, who originated the recipe in the village of Cheddar, Somersetshire, admit is the finest in the world.

How did the flavour of Canadian Cheddar become so popular? Better grazing pastures and high quality bacterial culture, often a well-kept secret, contributed to the making of superior Cheddar, but the individual touch of the family cheese makers elevated Cheddar production to the level of a specialized craft.

Cheddar production in Ontario increased dramatically around the mid-nineteenth century and, in 1904, Canada shipped 106 million kg of Cheddar to the United Kingdom. Proud cheesemakers produced giant round cheeses to show off their vintage products at world fairs. The "Canadian Mite" weighing in at 10 000 kg, was made for exhibit at the Chicago World's Fair in 1893. The Mite was so heavy that the railway car transporting it to Chicago broke from its weight and, once installed for display, the giant cheese crashed through the floor!

This story still amuses me when I think of the 100 kg of Cheddar used to develop the recipes in this book.

My thanks again to my family and friends with whom I shared many memorable Cheddar evenings.

Helpful Hints

- When refrigerating Cheddar, use within 4 weeks.

- Refrigerate Cheddar in its original wrapper. After cutting, cover in plastic wrap or foil, or store in an airtight container.

- A very large piece of Cheddar may be stored in a cool place for 1 month or longer when the cut side is protected with a coat of melted paraffin.

- When freezing Cheddar, cut no more than 1" (2.5 cm) thick, in 1 lb (500 g) portions. Wrap portions in foil and label.

- Use previously frozen Cheddar for cooking only, as thawing produces a crumbly texture.

- Grate Cheddar in advance for cooking. Portion and freeze in plastic bags or airtight containers, and use as required. (It is not necessary to thaw Cheddar first.)

- When grating Cheddar with a food processor, best results are achieved when Cheddar is chilled and firm.

- Hardened Cheddar is still suitable for grating and use in cooking.

- Do not wrap Cheddar pieces with other cheeses, as flavours may mingle.

- When substituting old or extra-old Cheddar for mild or medium in a recipe, cut back quantity to taste.

- Cheddar tastes best when eaten at room temperature (about 68°F or 20°C).

- To retain best flavour, do not bring large pieces of Cheddar to room temperature time and time again. Estimate portions per person. For example, when serving Cheddar with crackers, calculate approximately ¼-½ lb (125-250 g) Cheddar per person.

- Avoid strongly flavoured crackers when serving Cheddar.

- Suitable fruits to serve with Cheddar are grapes, pineapple, apple, pear, dates and figs.

Soups, Appetizers & Light Meals

Apple Cheddar Soup

Makes 4-6 servings

large apple	1, thinly sliced
medium onion	1, thinly sliced
butter	¼ cup (50 mL)
all-purpose flour	2 Tbsp (25 mL)
hot chicken broth	2 cups (500 mL) (dissolve 2 bouillon cubes in boiling water)
10% or 18% cream	1 cup (250 mL)
medium or old Cheddar	2 cups (500 mL), grated
paprika	¼ tsp (1 mL)
Worcestershire sauce	2 dashes
white pepper	⅛ tsp (0.5 mL)

Garnish: Slivers of unpeeled red apple or fresh parsley, finely chopped

In a 2-qt (2 L) Teflon-coated saucepan, sauté apple and onion in butter until just cooked (apple should not become mushy). Add flour, stir and cook for 1 minute.

Add hot chicken broth, a little at a time. Stir until smooth and thickened. Add cream and cook until heated through (do not boil). Add Cheddar, a quarter at a time, stirring until melted. Add seasonings. Ladle soup into heated bowls. Garnish as desired.

Cheddar Soup Printanière

butter	¼ cup (50 mL)
all-purpose flour	¼ cup (50 mL), unsifted
hot chicken broth	3 cups (750 mL) (dissolve 2 bouillon cubes in boiling water)
clove garlic	1, finely minced
green onion	½-1 cup (125-250 mL), finely chopped
celery	1 cup (250 mL), finely diced
carrot	1 cup (250 mL), finely diced
egg yolk	1
10% or 18% cream	½ cup (125 mL)
Parmesan cheese	2 Tbsp (25 mL), freshly grated
mild or medium Cheddar	1½ cups (375 mL), grated
cayenne pepper & nutmeg	pinch each
salt and pepper	To taste

Garnish: Fresh parsley, finely chopped, or croutons

In a heavy 2-qt (2 L) saucepan, melt butter. Add flour and cook for 3 minutes over low heat. Add hot broth, a little at a time, and stir until smooth and thickened. Add garlic, onion, celery, carrot and simmer covered until vegetables are just cooked (approx. 15 minutes).

In a small bowl, beat egg yolk lightly with cream. Pour ½ cup (125 mL) hot soup into yolk mixture and whisk to combine. Pour mixture back into saucepan in a slow stream, stirring continuously until thickened (do not boil). Add Parmesan, then Cheddar one third at a time, until Cheddar is melted. Add seasonings. Ladle soup into heated bowls. Garnish with parsley or croutons and serve.

Cream of Broccoli & Cheddar Soup

Makes 4-6 servings

water	4 cups (1 L)
fresh broccoli	2 bunches, washed & coarsely chopped
bay leaf	1
chicken or vegetable bouillon cubes	2
mild or medium Cheddar	2 cups (500 mL), grated
10% or 18% cream	1½-2 cups (375-500 mL)
soya sauce or Worcestershire sauce	½ tsp (2 mL)
dried marjoram	¼ tsp (1 mL)
nutmeg	⅛ tsp (0.5 mL)
hot pepper sauce	4 dashes
salt & pepper	*To taste*

Garnish: Croutons

In a 3-qt (3 L) saucepan, combine water, broccoli, bay leaf and bouillon. Bring to a boil, and simmer covered until very tender. Remove bay leaf, and purée broccoli together with broth in batches in a blender or food processor. There should be 5-6 cups (1.25 to 1.5 L) of purée. Transfer purée back to saucepan. Heat to just below boiling. Add Cheddar, one quarter at a time, stirring until melted. Add cream and seasonings. Heat through (do not boil). Ladle into heated bowls. Garnish with croutons.

Cream of Cauliflower & Cheddar Soup

Makes 4-6 servings

cauliflower	1, medium-large
water	2 cups (500 mL)
celery	½ cup (125 mL), chopped (include leaves)
onion	½ cup (125 mL), chopped
chicken bouillon cube	1
butter	2 Tbsp (25 mL)
all-purpose flour	2 Tbsp (25 mL)
10% cream	1 cup (250 mL)
Cheddar	1 cup (250 mL), grated
seasoned salt	½ tsp (2 mL)
Worcestershire sauce	¼ tsp (1 mL)
celery salt, pepper, & nutmeg	⅛ tsp each (0.5 mL)

Garnish: Fresh parsley, finely chopped

Trim cauliflower and break into small flowerettes. In a 2-qt (2 L) saucepan, add water, cauliflower, celery and onion. Bring to a boil. Add bouillon cube and stir to dissolve. Reduce heat and simmer covered until vegetables are very tender. Drain, reserving broth. Remove 1 cup (250 mL) flowerettes and set aside. Purée vegetables in batches in food processor or blender.

In a 3-qt (3 L) saucepan melt butter. Stir in flour and cook for 1 minute. Add reserved broth and stir over medium heat until smooth and thickened. Stir in purée, then cream. Heat to just below boiling. Add Cheddar, stirring until melted. Add seasonings and reserved flowerettes. Ladle into heated bowls. Garnish with fresh parsley and serve.

Cream of Celery & Leek Soup

Makes 4-6 servings

butter	¼ cup (50 mL)
celery	¾ lb (350 g), washed & sliced
leek	¾ lb (350 g), washed & sliced
hot chicken broth	3 cups (750 mL) (or 2 chicken bouillon cubes dissolved in boiling water)
parsley stems	10-15
bay leaf	1
10% or 18% cream	1 cup (250 mL)
mild or medium Cheddar	1 cup (250 mL), grated
salt & pepper	*To taste*
	Garnish: Fresh parsley or chives, chopped

In a 3-qt (3 L) saucepan, melt butter. Add celery and leek. Cover with a buttered round of waxed paper and lid. Sweat over medium heat for 10 minutes. Add hot chicken broth. Tie parsley stems and bay leaf together with a string and add. Bring to a boil and simmer covered for 30 minutes. Discard parsley stems and bay leaf.

Purée mixture in batches in blender or food processor. Return mixture to saucepan and add cream. Heat to just below boiling, then add Cheddar, stirring until melted. Season with salt and pepper to taste. Ladle soup into heated bowls. Garnish with parsley or chives.

VARIATION

Cream of Endive & Leek Soup—Substitute halved, washed and sliced Belgian endive for celery.

Cheesey Corn Chowder

Makes 4-6 servings

bacon	4 slices, chopped
onion	½-¾ cup (125-175 mL), finely chopped
large potato	1, diced in ¼" (6mm) cubes
water	2 cups (500 mL)
salt	1 tsp (5 mL)
bay leaf	1
tomato paste	2 Tbsp (25 mL)
creamed corn	1 x 14-oz (398 mL) can
mild or medium Cheddar	1½ cups (375 mL), grated
fresh parsley	1 Tbsp (25 mL), finely chopped
pepper	⅛ tsp (0.5 mL)
Worcestershire sauce	⅛ tsp (0.5 mL)
heavy cream	½ cup (125 mL)

Garnish: Green onion or sweet red pepper, finely chopped

In a 2-qt (2 L) Teflon-coated saucepan, fry bacon until semi-crisp. Add onion and sauté until onion is transparent. Add potato, water, salt and bay leaf. Bring to a boil, then stir in tomato paste. Cover and simmer 15 minutes, until potato is tender. With back of spoon or potato masher, mash slightly in saucepan. Add corn and cook until heated through. Add Cheddar, a third at a time, stirring until melted. Stir in seasonings and cream. Heat (do not boil). Ladle soup into heated bowls. Garnish with green onion or sweet red pepper.

Cream of Roquefort & Cheddar Soup

Makes 3-4 servings

Roquefort cheese	4 oz (125 g)
milk	2 cups (500 mL), warmed
egg yolks	2, lightly beaten
18% cream	½ cup (125 mL)
Cheddar	1 cup (250 mL), grated

Garnish: Halved, unpeeled cucumber slices, chopped parsley or dash of paprika

In a blender, purée Roquefort with warm milk. Transfer to a 1-qt (1 L) saucepan and heat to just below boiling. In a small bowl, combine egg yolks with cream. Whisk 1 cup (250 mL) of Roquefort milk gradually into egg mixture. Whisk the mixture back into saucepan in a slow stream. Stir soup while heating through. Blend in Cheddar, stirring until melted. Ladle into heated bowls. Garnish as desired.

VARIATION

Chill soup and use as a tasty salad dressing or raw vegetable dip.

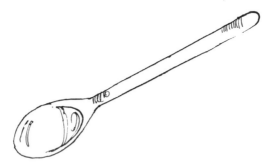

Cream of Rutabaga & Cheddar Soup

Makes 4-6 servings

Yellow Turnip Purée: In a medium saucepan, cook ½ yellow turnip, peeled and cubed, in 2 cups (500 mL) of water plus 1 chicken bouillon cube. When very tender, purée in blender or food processor until smooth. Set aside.

butter	¼ cup (50 mL)
all-purpose flour	¼ cup (50 mL), unsifted
milk	2 cups (500 mL)
turnip purée	as prepared above
mild or medium Cheddar	2 cups (500 mL), grated
Worcestershire sauce	1 tsp (5 mL)
celery salt	¼ tsp (1 mL)
nutmeg	⅛ tsp (0.5 mL)
white pepper	⅛ tsp (0.5 mL)

Garnish: Fresh parsley, chives or celery leaves, chopped

In a 3-qt (3 L) Teflon-coated saucepan, melt butter. Add flour and cook, stirring for 2 minutes. Slowly whisk in milk, stirring continuously to form a smooth sauce. Add yellow turnip purée and heat to just below boiling. Add grated Cheddar, a quarter at a time, stirring until melted. Add seasonings. Ladle into heated bowls. Garnish as desired.

11

Cheddar Soup Florentine

Makes 4-6 servings

Spinach Purée: Wash well 1 x 10-oz (284-g) bag of fresh spinach. Place wet leaves in large saucepan, and cook over medium heat until tender (approx. 10 minutes). Crumble 2 chicken bouillon cubes into hot mixture and stir to dissolve. Purée mixture in blender or food processor. Set aside.

butter	3 Tbsp (50 mL)
onion	½ cup (125 mL), finely chopped
all-purpose flour	1 Tbsp (15 mL)
milk	2 cups (500 mL)
spinach purée	as prepared above
egg yolks	2
18% cream	½ cup (125 mL)
medium or old Cheddar	1-1½ cups (250-375 mL), grated
soya sauce	4 dashes
nutmeg	pinch
ginger	pinch
salt & pepper	*To taste*

Garnish: Chopped hard-cooked egg or chopped celery leaves

In a 2-qt (2 L) saucepan, melt butter. Add onion and sauté until transparent and golden. Sprinkle flour over mixture and cook for 1 minute. Stir in milk and cook until heated through. Add spinach purée and heat to just below boiling. In a small bowl, beat yolks lightly with cream. Pour ½ cup (125 mL) hot soup into yolk mixture and whisk to combine. Pour mixture back into saucepan in a slow stream, stirring continuously until thickened (do not boil). Add Cheddar, a third at a time, stirring until melted. Stir in seasonings. Ladle soup into heated bowls. Garnish and serve.

Confetti Cheese Ball

Makes 2-4" (10 cm) balls or 1-8" (20 cm) log

onion	2 Tbsp (25 mL), finely minced
green pepper	3 Tbsp (50 mL), finely chopped
pimiento-stuffed olives	10 sliced
sweet pickle relish	2 Tbsp (25 mL)
eggs	2 hard-cooked, chopped
salt	¼ tsp (1 mL)
pepper	⅛ tsp (0.5 mL)
Wheatsworth or soda crackers	½ cup (125 mL), crushed
mild or medium Cheddar	2 cups (500 mL), grated
real mayonnaise	¼ cup (50 mL)

Garnish: Finely chopped fresh parsley, walnut halves or pecan halves
Assorted crackers

In a medium bowl, mix all ingredients well. Form into 2-4" (10 cm) balls or one log. Roll balls or log in finely chopped parsley or decorate with walnut or pecan halves. Cover and chill several hours, until firm. Remove from refrigerator ½ hour before serving with assorted crackers.

VARIATION

Delicious when rolled in toasted pumpkin seeds.

HINT

Cover cheese log with waxed paper and roll to form a smooth log. In storing balls, line a foil meat pie form with waxed paper. Place hand-formed ball in centre and cover. At serving time, lift out ball and transfer to platter. (Also a handy method of transporting cheese balls to a party.)

Molded Cheese Ring

medium or old Cheddar	1 lb (500 g), finely grated
pecans or walnuts	1 cup (250 mL), finely chopped
small onion	1, finely grated
plain whole or skim milk yogurt	1 cup (250 mL), drained 4-8 hours
sugar	1 Tbsp (15 mL)
cayenne pepper	*To taste*
assorted crackers	
strawberry or raspberry preserves	

Lightly oil a 4-cup (1 L) ring mold. In a medium bowl, combine all ingredients well (except crackers and preserves) and pack into mold. Refrigerate several hours or overnight. Unmold, and serve with assorted crackers and strawberry or raspberry preserves in the centre.

HINT

Yogurt will drain more quickly in a wire-mesh sieve. To drain; line a sieve with cheesecloth or J-Cloth, and place over a bowl. Pour yogurt into sieve and drain 4-8 hours.

Cheddar Potato Peel Crisps

        potato peels
        salt & pepper
          Cheddar   grated

Reserve the peels from baked, raw or boiled potatoes.

   Cut peels ⅛" (3 mm) thick and into 3 x 1" (7½ x 2½ cm) strips. Arrange the strips closely together in one layer in a buttered cookie pan. Sprinkle lightly with salt and pepper. Bake in a 450°F (230°C) oven for 10-25 minutes, according to the type of peel, or until very crisp. Sprinkle the peels with Cheddar and broil briefly until lightly browned. Separate peels and serve hot.

HINT

Baked peels cook in 7-10 minutes. Raw peels cook in 15-25 minutes. Boiled peels cook in 20-25 minutes.

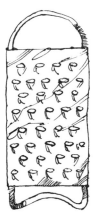

Mushroom Bacon Wraps

Cheddar spread: Mix until smooth and well blended; 2 cups (500 mL) grated Cheddar, ¼ cup (50 mL) finely chopped onion, ¼ cup (50 mL) butter or real mayonnaise, 1 tsp (5 mL) Worcestershire sauce, ¼ tsp (1 mL) garlic powder and ⅛ tsp (0.5 mL) pepper.

large mushroom caps	cleaned, stems removed
bacon strips	cut in half
toothpicks	

One or several of the following:

smoked oysters	drained and halved if large
mussels	fresh or smoked
baby clams	
salami	small cubes
Polish sausage, kielbasa or smoked sausage	

hot crusty French bread or toast triangles

Press a generous amount of Cheddar spread into each mushroom cap. Place a piece of fish or sausage on top. Wrap each mushroom in bacon and secure with toothpick. Arrange on rimmed cookie sheet and bake in a 400°F (200°C) oven for 20 minutes until bacon and mushrooms are cooked. Serve hot with crusty French bread or toast triangles.

HINT

For extra-crisp bacon, drain bacon fat away after 20 minutes and broil briefly. Mushrooms wraps may be prepared in advance and refrigerated.

Hot Crab Dip

Makes 6-8 servings

butter	2 Tbsp (25 mL), softened
cream cheese	8 oz (250-g pkg), softened
Cheddar	1 cup (250 mL), grated
snow crab meat	1 x 5-oz can (142 g can), rinsed, drained & flaked

OR

frozen snow crab meat	1 x 7-oz (200-g) pkg, thawed, rinsed, drained & flaked
prepared horseradish	4 tsp (20 mL)
green onion (including tops)	1-2, finely chopped
Worcestershire sauce	½-1 tsp (2-5 mL)

In the bowl of an electric mixer or food processor, beat butter, cream cheese and Cheddar until well blended. Add crab meat and remaining ingredients. Pack mixture into two earthenware onion soup bowls. Heat in a 375°F (190°C) oven for 20-30 minutes, until hot and bubbly. Serve with crackers and bread sticks.

VARIATION

Hot Crab Tartlets—Fully pre-bake miniature tart shells. Spoon a little crab mixture into each and bake in a 375°F (190°C) oven for 15 minutes.
Bread casings may be substituted for tart shells; remove crusts from pre-sliced brown or white bread and place in buttered muffin cups. Toast in a 375°F (190°C) oven for 15 minutes. Fill with crab mixture and continue baking until heated through.
Hot Crab Puffs—Pre-bake miniature cream puff shells. Fill with crab mixture and heat in oven.

HINT

This dip is excellent cold as a spread. Heat one earthenware bowl to serve hot, and chill the second.

Cheddar Quiche Squares

Makes approx. 35

Pre-baked pastry:
Prepare a plain or Cheddar double-crust pastry recipe. Line an 11" x 7" (27.5 x 17.5 cm) rimmed cookie pan with pastry. Cover bottom crust with waxed paper, weigh down with dry beans, and pre-bake in a 400°F (200°C) oven for 10 minutes. Remove waxed paper and beans. Cool while preparing filling.

pre-baked pastry	
bacon	½ lb (250 g)
large onion	1, chopped
Cheddar	1 lb (500 g), grated
eggs	5
sour cream	2 cups (500 mL)
salt, pepper & cayenne	*To taste*

Fry bacon until crisp, then drain and crumble. Sprinkle evenly over bottom of pre-baked crust. Reserve a little bacon fat and in it sauté onion until transparent. Distribute evenly over crust. Sprinkle grated Cheddar over bacon and onion. In a medium bowl, beat eggs lightly together with sour cream and seasonings. Pour over Cheddar and bake in a 400°F (200°C) oven for 20-30 minutes or until set and lightly browned. Cool 10 minutes and cut into 35/2 x 2" squares (35/5 x 5 cm).

VARIATION

Chopped green onion may be substituted for fried onion. For infants, omit bacon and onion, and substitute dashes of nutmeg for salt and pepper. Freeze in small squares and reheat a few pieces at a time for meals.

HINT

Freezes well. Cut into squares when cooled and freeze in layers between waxed paper, in plastic airtight containers.

Artichoke Mushroom Squares

Makes approx. 35/2 x 2" (5 x 5 cm) squares

marinated artichoke hearts	1 x 6-oz (170-mL) jar
mushrooms	1 cup (250 mL), sliced
small onions	2, finely chopped
mild or medium Cheddar	2 cups (500 mL), grated
eggs	4, lightly beaten
fresh parsley	1 Tbsp (15 mL), chopped
salt	½ tsp (2 mL)
garlic powder	¼ tsp (1 mL)
dried oregano	¼ tsp (1 mL)
hot pepper sauce	*To taste*
dry breadcrumbs	½ cup (125 mL)

Drain and chop artichokes, reserving the marinade. Sauté mushrooms and onions in artichoke marinade until onions are transparent. In a medium bowl, mix beaten eggs, chopped artichokes, onion and mushroom mixture and seasonings. Stir in breadcrumbs. Spread mixture in a buttered 11 x 7" (27.5 x 17.5 cm) rimmed cookie pan. Bake in a 325°F (160°C) oven for 30 minutes. Cool 5 minutes and cut into 35 squares of 2 x 2" (5 x 5 cm).

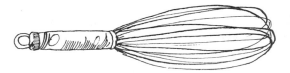

Versatile Cheddar Pastries

Pastry:

all-purpose flour	4 cups (1 L), unsifted
margarine	2 cups (500 mL), chilled
egg yolks	4, lightly beaten
sour cream	1 cup (250 mL)
Cheddar	3-4 cups (750-1000 mL), grated

Glaze: Cream, or 1 egg yolk beaten with 2 Tbsp (25 mL) milk

Pastry: In a large bowl, cut margarine into flour with a pastry blender until mixture resembles coarse crumbs. In a small bowl, beat egg yolks with sour cream. Add egg mixture all at once to flour mixture and stir with a fork to moisten. With hands, form into a ball, kneading briefly to make a smooth dough. Divide dough into 4 equal portions. Wrap each portion in waxed paper and chill for one hour.

On a floured surface, roll out one portion into a large rectangle. Sprinkle with ¾-1 cup (175-250 mL) Cheddar. Fold over several times and re-roll until Cheddar is well incorporated. Repeat process with remaining portions (incorporating ¾-1 cup or 175-250 mL Cheddar into each portion). Prepare pastries as directed in VARIATIONS.

Place 1" (2.5 cm) apart on ungreased baking sheet. Brush with glaze and bake all pastries in a 400°F (200°C) oven for 10 minutes or until golden.

VARIATIONS

Caraway or Sesame Seed Crisps—Roll 1-2 tsp (5-10 mL) caraway or sesame seeds into 1 portion of dough. Roll dough ¼" (6 mm) thick. Cut into various shapes with cookie cutters.

Wiener Roll-Ups—Roll pastry ¼" (6 mm) thick. Cut into ½" (1.25 cm) strips, approx. 6" (15 cm) long. Brush lightly with prepared nippy mustard sauce. Spiral around canned cocktail wieners.

HINT

These pastries freeze well (baked or unbaked).

Savoury Cheddar Charlotte

Makes 8-12 servings

white bread	2-3 slices, crusts removed
whole wheat bread	2-3 slices, crusts removed
soft butter	
cream cheese	1 x 4-oz pkg (125 g), softened
mild or medium Cheddar	1 cup (250 mL), grated
eggs	3, separated
creamed cottage cheese	1 cup (250 mL)
salt	¼-½ tsp (1-2 mL)
white pepper	⅛-¼ tsp (0.5-1 mL)
Dijon-style mustard	½ tsp (2 mL)
sugar	1 tsp (5 mL)
unflavoured gelatin	1 envelope, softened in ¼ cup (50 mL) cold water
pimiento	¼ cup (50 mL), finely chopped

OR

green pepper	½ cup (125 mL), finely chopped

Garnish: Watercress, cherry tomatoes, green pepper strips

Butter a 5-6 cup (1.25-1.5 L) pudding or charlotte mold. Trim bread. Butter one side only and cut into strips. Arrange strips in alternate colours on sides of mold, buttered side in. In the bowl of an electric mixer or food processor beat together until very smooth, cream cheese and Cheddar. Add egg yolks and process until smooth. Transfer mixture to a large bowl. Stir in cottage cheese, salt, pepper, mustard and sugar.

In a small saucepan, sprinkle gelatin over the cold water. Stir over low heat until gelatin is dissolved (approx. 3 minutes). Immediately add to cheese mixture. Beat egg whites until stiff and fold into cheese mixture. Spoon into prepared mold. Cover mold with plastic wrap and refrigerate at least 3-4 hours. Unmold and serve on a bed of watercress with cherry tomatoes and green pepper strips.

VARIATION

Omit mustard and pimiento or green pepper. Add 1 tsp (5 mL) finely grated lemon rind. Serve charlotte on a bed of bibb or Boston lettuce, accompanied by a bowl of fresh fruit salad.

Asparagus Cheddar Rolls

Makes 40-48 appetizers

Cheddar	2 cups (500 mL), grated
onion	¼ cup (50 mL), finely chopped
butter or real mayonnaise	¼ cup (50 mL)
Worcestershire sauce	1 tsp (5 mL)
garlic powder	¼ tsp (1 mL)
pepper	⅛ tsp (0.5 mL)
asparagus spears	1 x 14-oz (398 mL) can, drained
sandwich bread	1 loaf, thinly sliced
toothpicks	
butter	½ cup (50 mL), melted

Mix until smooth and well blended; Cheddar, onion, mayonnaise, Worcestershire sauce, garlic powder and pepper. Drain asparagus spears. Trim crusts from bread and spread a generous amount of Cheddar mixture on each piece. Place one or two (if thin) asparagus spears, diagonally or lengthwise on each bread slice (when using two spears, have one tip at either end). Make a roll and join with toothpicks. Place rolls on greased, rimmed baking sheet. Brush the outside with melted butter. Bake in a 400°F (200°C) oven for 15-20 minutes. Cut in half and serve hot.

VARIATION

Substitute drained and halved marinated artichoke hearts for asparagus. Make Cheddar Ham Rolls by placing thin slices of ham in centre of bread.

HINT

Serve uncut as a sandwich to accompany a soup. Leftover filling may be stored in the refrigerator for several days and spread on toast (a tasty spread for bacon and tomato sandwiches or ham sandwiches).

Cheddar Reubens

Makes 8 servings

sauerkraut	1 x 14-oz (398 mL) can, drained & rinsed (approx. 2 cups or 500 mL)
rye bread	8-10 slices
butter	softened
prepared nippy mustard sauce	*To taste*
corned beef	16-20, thin slices
medium or old Cheddar	½ lb (250 g), thinly sliced

Drain and rinse sauerkraut. Squeeze moisture out with hands. Lightly butter rye bread and spread with mustard sauce. Place two pieces of corned beef on top. Heap generous portion of sauerkraut on each slice. Top with slices of Cheddar. Broil until heated through and tops are browned and bubbly.

HINT

For a milder sauerkraut flavour, place drained sauerkraut in pot of cold water and boil for 10 minutes. Drain and squeeze out moisture.

SERVING SUGGESTION

Miniature Cheddar Reubens—Buy party rye bread slices and make in miniature.

Tuna Salad in Pita Pockets

Makes 6 servings

tuna	1 x 6½-oz (184 mL) can, drained & shredded
cherry tomatoes	1 cup (250 mL), halved
green pepper	½ cup (125 mL), chopped
red or green onion	¼ cup (50 mL), finely chopped
black olives	½ cup (125 mL), sliced
Cheddar	1 cup (250 mL), diced
oil & vinegar salad dressing mixed with 1 tsp (5 mL) crumbled sweet basil	½ cup (125 mL)
whole wheat or white pita bread	6

In a medium bowl, combine ingredients for filling. Toss with salad dressing. Stuff mixture into pita bread pockets.

HINT

For outings, put stuffing in air-tight containers and stuff pockets just before serving.

Stuffed French Loaf

Makes 4-6 servings

French stick	1 x 12" loaf (30 cm)
butter	¼ cup (50 mL), melted
garlic clove	1, crushed
crushed pineapple	1 cup (250 mL), undrained
mild Cheddar	1 cup (250 mL), grated
raisins	½ cup (125 mL)
celery	¼ cup (50 mL), finely chopped
walnuts or pecans	¼ cup (50 mL), chopped
dry mustard	pinch
salt & pepper	*To taste*

Cut bread in half horizontally. Scoop out centre of each half, making soft crumbs. In a medium bowl, combine butter and garlic. Add pineapple, Cheddar, raisins, celery, nuts and seasonings. Mix lightly and add enough breadcrumbs to make a stuffing which contains no excess moisture. Heap into French-stick shells and sandwich together. With a sharp serrated knife, cut loaf into 1" (2½ cm) slices, taking care to leave bottoms attached. Wrap in foil and heat in a 375°F (190°C) oven for 15-20 minutes, until heated through. Cut in slices.

VARIATION

Omit raisins and substitute ½ cup (125 mL) washed, drained and sliced canned water chestnuts, plus ¼ cup (50 mL) finely chopped green pepper.

HINT

This loaf is also delicious chilled and served at room temperature. Take to a picnic or other outings.

Cheddar Griddle Cakes

Makes 2-3 servings

egg	1
buttermilk or whole milk	½ cup (125 mL)
Cheddar	¾ cup (175 mL), grated
all-purpose flour	6 Tbsp (90 mL)
baking powder	1 tsp (5 mL)
salt	¼ tsp (1 mL)
lemon rind	½ tsp (2 mL), finely grated
nutmeg	⅛ tsp (0.5 mL)

In a medium bowl, beat egg with buttermilk or milk. Add Cheddar, flour, baking powder, salt and flavourings. On a pre-heated, oiled griddle, pour batter by heaping tablespoons for each cake. When bubbles form on the top, and undersides are browned, turn cakes and brown the other side. Transfer to a warmed platter. Serve with maple syrup or applesauce.

VARIATION

Omit lemon rind and substitute ¼ cup (50 mL) finely chopped green onion. Serve with fresh garden tomatoes fried in a small amount of oil and sprinkled with baby dill.

3-Cheese Pudding

Makes 4-6 servings

eggs	3, lightly beaten
milk	½ cup (125 mL)
creamed cottage cheese	½ cup (125 mL)
Cheddar	½ lb (250 g), cut in ½" (1.25 cm) cubes
cream cheese	4 oz (125-g pkg), cut in ½" (1.25 cm) cubes
all-purpose flour	¼ cup (50 ml), unsifted
baking powder	½ tsp (2 mL)
hot green chili peppers	1 x 4-oz (114-mL) can, drained & chopped

In a medium bowl, combine eggs, milk, cottage cheese, Cheddar and white cream cheese. Combine lightly. Stir in flour mixed with baking powder. Fold in chopped chili peppers. Pour into a buttered 8" (2 L) square baking pan. Bake in a 350°F (180°C) oven, for 45-50 minutes or until puffy and golden. Cool 5 minutes. Cut and serve.

HINT

Calorie watchers may omit cream cheese.

SERVING SUGGESTION

Serve with chili sauce, crusty bread and salad.

Mexican Omelette

Makes 2-4 servings

olive oil	2 Tbsp (25 mL)
small onion	1, thinly sliced
green pepper	1, seeded & sliced
medium tomatoes	2, seeded & chopped
hot green chili peppers	1-2, finely chopped
salt & pepper	*To taste*
eggs	5, lightly beaten
Cheddar	½-¾ cup (125-175 mL), grated

Heat oil in a 12" (30 cm) oven-proof skillet. Add onion and sauté until transparent. Add green pepper and cook over low heat until tender-crisp. Increase heat to high and stir in chopped tomatoes and green chili peppers. Cook briefly until moisture evaporates. Sprinkle with salt and pepper. Reduce heat to low. Pour beaten eggs over mixture and cook until bottom sets. Sprinkle with Cheddar and place under broiler until puffed and lightly browned. Serve in wedges with crusty bread.

HINT

A Teflon-coated skillet may be made oven-proof by covering the handle with foil wrap.

Cheddar Ramekins

Makes 6 servings

butter	2 Tbsp (25 mL)
green onion	2 Tbsp (25 mL), finely chopped
fresh parsley	2 Tbsp (25 mL), finely chopped
mushrooms	2 cups (500 mL), thinly sliced
salt & pepper	*To taste*
milk	⅓ cup (75 mL)
eggs	2, separated
mild or medium Cheddar	1½ cups (375 mL), grated

In a small skillet, melt butter. Add green onion and parsley and sauté 1 minute. Add mushrooms and sauté until liquid has evaporated and mushrooms have browned slightly. Season with salt and pepper. Spoon 1 heaping tablespoon of the mixture into each ramekin dish. In a 1-qt (1 L) heavy saucepan, combine milk, egg yolks and Cheddar. Cook and stir mixture over gentle heat until cheese is melted. Beat egg whites until stiff but not dry. Fold beaten whites into cheese mixture. Divide mixture evenly among the 6 buttered ramekins. Arrange dishes on baking sheet and bake in a 375°F (190°C) oven for 12-15 minutes until cheese mixture is well puffed and golden. Serve at once.

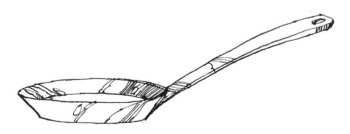

Baked Chili Rellenos

Makes 2 servings

hot green chili peppers	1 x 4-oz (114-mL) can
Cheddar	½ lb (250 g), thinly sliced
egg	1
milk	1 cup (250 mL)
all-purpose flour	¼ cup (50 mL), unsifted
salt	¼ tsp (1 mL)
chili powder	⅛ tsp (0.5 mL)

Butter an 8" (2 L) square pan, or a loaf pan. Seed chili peppers and cut into large squares. Arrange on bottom of pan. Layer slices of Cheddar on top. In a small bowl, beat egg with milk, flour, salt, and chili powder. Pour over Cheddar and bake in a 350°F (180°C) oven for 40-45 minutes, or until centre is set. Cool 10 minutes, cut and serve.

HINT

For a milder flavour, substitute half chili pepper, half chopped sweet pimiento for chili pepper.

SERVING SUGGESTION

Cut into squares and serve with tostada shells, or make Chili Relleno Pie by layering mixture and baking in a pre-baked pie shell. Serve with salad for lunch.

Farmhouse Fondue

Makes 4 servings

garlic clove	1
mild or medium Cheddar	½ lb (250 g), grated
mild or medium Gouda cheese	½ lb (250 g), grated
cornstarch	1 Tbsp (15 mL)
butter	1 Tbsp (15 mL)
buttermilk or whole milk	1 cup (250 mL)
lemon juice	1 tsp (5 mL)
sugar	1 tsp (5 mL)
salt (optional)	½ tsp (2 mL)
dry mustard	¼ tsp (1 mL)
nutmeg	⅛ tsp (0.5 mL)
cayenne pepper	⅛ tsp (0.5 mL)
allspice	pinch
crusty French stick	1 loaf, cut into large cubes

Rub inside of cheese fondue pot with a cut garlic clove. Toss Cheddar and Gouda together with cornstarch in fondue pot. Add remaining ingredients, except bread, and heat very gently, stirring continuously until cheese melts and mixture thickens. Do not boil. Serve hot with a basket of bread cubes to spear on fondue forks for dunking.

VARIATION

Crab Cheddar Fondue—Add 1 x 6½-oz (184 mL) can of snow crab meat, drained, rinsed and shredded. Thin out fondue with additional milk if necessary, or add sherry to taste. Instead of milk, ale or Woodpecker's English Cider (or non-alcoholic cider) may be substituted. Also, 1 lb (500 g) Cheddar may be substituted for the Gouda/Cheddar combination.

SERVING SUGGESTION

Red and green pepper strips, apple slices and broccoli or cauliflower buds, steamed until tender-crisp, make excellent dippers.

31

Broiled Rabbit (Rarebit)

Makes 4 servings

bread	4 slices, toasted & lightly buttered
mild or medium Cheddar	½ lb (250 g), grated
cornstarch	1 Tbsp (15 mL)
Worcestershire sauce, Dijon-style mustard, grated onion, & prepared horseradish	1 tsp (5 mL) each
apple cider or juice	¼ cup (50 mL)
egg yolk	1
salt & pepper	*To taste*

Toast bread and arrange slices close together in a lightly buttered, shallow baking dish. Combine all other ingredients except egg yolk, salt and pepper in top of a double boiler. Heat mixture until Cheddar begins to melt. Stir continuously until the rabbit is a smooth sauce. Remove from heat and beat in egg yolk. Return to low heat or over the double boiler and continue cooking for 1 minute, until rabbit is thickened. Season with salt and pepper. Pour on toast and broil until browned. Serve hot.

VARIATIONS

Golden Buck — Top each toast slice with a poached egg before pouring on rabbit sauce.
Yorkshire Buck — Top each toast slice with 3 slices of crisp bacon, then a poached egg, before pouring on rabbit sauce.
Layer cooked asparagus spears, braised celery or Belgian endive on toast, before pouring on rabbit sauce.
Layer slices of hard-cooked eggs or tomato on toast before pouring over rabbit sauce.

Individual Cheddar Soufflés in Patty Shells

Makes 8 servings

frozen patty shells	8
butter	2 Tbsp (25 mL)
all-purpose flour	2 Tbsp (25 mL)
milk	½ cup (125 mL)
Dijon-style mustard	1 tsp (5 mL)
cayenne pepper	pinch
eggs	2, separated
old Cheddar	½ cup (125 mL), grated
salt	⅛ tsp (0.5 mL)
cream of tartar	dash

Bake frozen patty shells as directed on package. Remove tops and discard moist centres. Melt butter in a 1-qt (1 L) heavy saucepan. Add flour and stir for one minute to make a roux. Slowly add milk, stirring continuously to make a thick, smooth sauce (sauce should leave sides of pan). Add mustard and cayenne pepper. Remove from heat and beat in egg yolks. Add grated Cheddar and stir until well combined.

In a separate bowl, beat egg whites with salt and cream of tarter until stiff peaks form. Fold into cheese mixture. Place a heaping tablespoon of soufflé mixture in each patty shell (fill right to the top). Bake in a 375°F (190°C) oven for 15-20 minutes, until puffy and golden brown on top. Serve immediately.

VARIATION

Tomato Soufflés—Cut tops from 8 firm, ripe tomatoes. Scoop out pulp, sprinkle with salt and invert on paper towels for 30 minutes. Dry inside and fill with soufflé mixture. Bake as directed above.

SERVING SUGGESTION

Serve with buttered asparagus, or broccoli with lemon butter and garden tomato slices, sprinkled with chopped fresh baby dill.

Ham & Cheddar Gnocchi

Makes 2-4 servings

milk	1½ cups (375 mL)
farina (cream of wheat)	½ cup (125 mL)
butter	1 Tbsp (15 mL)
Cheddar	½ cup (125 mL), grated
egg yolk	1
seasoned salt	¼ tsp (1 mL)
Worcestershire sauce	4 dashes
nutmeg	pinch
cooked ham	½ cup (125 mL), finely chopped
fresh parsley	¼ cup (50 mL), finely chopped
green onion	¼ cup (50 mL), finely chopped

Lightly butter an 8" (2 L) square pan. In a medium saucepan, heat milk
slightly. Sprinkle in farina and cook over medium heat, stirring until
thickened (approx. 5 minutes). Stir in butter, Cheddar, egg yolk and
seasonings. Add ham, parsley and green onion. Spread evenly in prepared pan. Chill until firm (2-3 hours). Butter a shallow baking pan. Cut
chilled mixture into squares or roll into 1" (2.5 cm) balls. Place balls in
baking pan or arrange squares slightly overlapping. Sprinkle with additional Cheddar. Broil casserole 4-6" (10-15 cm) from heat until hot and
golden.

HINT

Gnocchi make delicious soup dumplings. Roll into balls and drop into
boiling soup. Simmer 5 minutes and serve.

NOTE

Cream of wheat may be purchased in whole wheat form also.

Main Dishes

Stuffed Jumbo Shells

Makes 4 servings

jumbo pasta shells	1 x 14-oz (375-g) pkg

Tomato Sauce:

canned tomatoes	2 x 28-oz (2 x 796-mL) cans, undrained
tomato paste	1 x 5½-oz (1 x 156-mL) can
Parmesan cheese, freshly grated	3 Tbsp (45 mL)
sugar	1 Tbsp (15 mL)
salt, dried oregano, & sweet basil	1 tsp each (5 mL)
pepper	¼ tsp (1 mL)

Filling:

small onion	1, finely chopped
large garlic clove	1, minced
olive oil	2 Tbsp (25 mL)
lean ground beef	1 lb (500 g)
fresh parsley	2 Tbsp (25 mL), finely chopped
salt	1 tsp (5 mL)
pepper & nutmeg	¼ each (1 mL)
white wine or white vermouth	¼ cup (50 mL)
Parmesan cheese	¼ cup (50 mL), freshly grated
dry breadcrumbs	¼ cup (50 mL)
Cheddar	1 cup (250 mL), grated
egg	1

Topping:

Cheddar	1 cup (250 mL), grated

Cook shells in boiling salted water for 20 minutes or until tender but firm. Stir gently while boiling. Drain, rinse, and drain again.

Tomato sauce: Combine ingredients in a saucepan. Heat until boiling and simmer for 20 minutes, uncovered.

Filling: Fry onion and garlic in oil until onion is transparent. Add ground beef and brown, stirring often to crumble meat. (If beef is medium-lean, drain off fat at this point.) Add seasonings. Add wine or vermouth and cook over medium heat until almost evaporated. Remove from heat and stir in Parmesan and breadcrumbs. Transfer mixture to a bowl to cool. When cooled stir in Cheddar and egg. Spread tomato sauce on bottom of 9 x 13" (3.5 L) casserole. Heap meat mixture into shells and place in a single layer on top of sauce. Cover casserole with lid or foil, and bake in a 375°F (190°C) oven for 30 minutes. Uncover, sprinkle with Cheddar Topping, and continue baking 10 minutes. Cool casserole 10 minutes before serving.

VARIATION

Cheese-Stuffed Jumbo Shells—Make cheese filling as in Cheese-Stuffed Canneloni.

HINT

To make 8 servings, add 1 egg plus 1 cup (250 mL) cooked, drained, squeezed and chopped spinach (fresh or frozen) to meat filling. Double tomato sauce and jumbo shells.

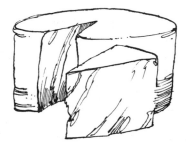

Cheese-Stuffed Canneloni

Makes 4 servings

Filling:

fresh spinach	1 x 10-oz (284 g) pkg
creamed cottage cheese	1 cup (250 mL)
Cheddar	1½ cups (375 mL), grated
onion	¼ cup (50 mL), finely chopped
fresh parsley	2 Tbsp (25 mL), finely chopped
dry breadcrumbs	2 Tbsp (25 mL)
celery salt	½ tsp (2 mL)
Worcestershire sauce	½ tsp (2 mL)
salt	¼ tsp (1 mL)
pepper	⅛ tsp (0.5 mL)
eggs	2, lightly beaten
uncooked canneloni shells	1 x 8-oz (250-g) pkg
canned tomatoes	1 x 28-oz (796-g) can, undrained

Topping

Cheddar	½ cup (125 mL), grated

Filling: Wash spinach. Cook, then drain and squeeze out moisture well. Chop spinach (you should have approx. 1 cup or 250 mL). In a medium bowl, combine spinach, cottage cheese, Cheddar, onion, parsley, breadcrumbs, seasonings and eggs. Stuff raw canneloni shells. Pour canned tomato evenly over the bottom of a 9 x 13" (3.5 L) casserole. Place canneloni in a single layer on top. Bake, covered, in a 350°F (180°C) oven for 50 minutes. Uncover casserole, sprinkle with Cheddar Topping, and continue baking 10 minutes. Cool 10 minutes before serving.

VARIATION

Meat-stuffed Canneloni—Follow recipe for meat filling in Stuffed Jumbo Shells. A nice addition is 1 cup (250 mL) chopped, cooked spinach to meat filling before stuffing. NOTE: The addition of spinach yields 6 servings, therefore it is important to use two casseroles and pour 1 x 28-oz (796-g) can tomatoes into each.

HINT

This casserole may be prepared in advance and refrigerated. However, pour canned tomatoes into casserole just before cooking.
     Cooked, frozen spinach may be substituted for fresh.

Macaroni Corned Beef Bake

Makes 4-6 servings

elbow macaroni	2 cups (500 mL)
butter	2 Tbsp (25 mL)
all-purpose flour	2 Tbsp (25 mL)
milk	1 cup (250 mL)
Cheddar	1 cup (250 mL), grated
salt	½ tsp (2 mL)
pepper	*To taste*
thick steak sauce	1 tsp (5 mL)
fresh parsley	2 Tbsp (25 mL), finely chopped
flakes of corned beef	1 x 6½-oz (184 mL) can, including liquid

Topping:

Cheddar	1 cup (250 mL), grated

Cook macaroni in boiling salted water until tender but firm.
Cheese Sauce: Melt butter, stir in flour and cook for 1 minute. Add milk plus liquid from corned beef gradually, stirring continuously to make a smooth sauce. Add Cheddar, stirring until melted. Season with salt, pepper, thick steak sauce and parsley.

Break corned beef into 1" (2.5 cm) chunks and fold into sauce together with cooked macaroni. Turn into buttered 2-qt (2 L) casserole and bake covered in a 350°F (180°C) oven for 20 minutes. Uncover, sprinkle with Cheddar Topping, and continue baking 10 minutes.

HINT

Canned flakes of chicken or ham may be substituted. Try out several pasta shapes for an attractive dish; e.g. tube pasta, small seashells, wagon wheels, spirals.

Chicken Broccoli Divan

Makes 4-6 servings

broccoli	1 bunch
water	2 cups (500 mL)
salt	1 tsp (5 mL)
chicken bouillon cube	1

Sauce:

butter	¼ cup (50 mL)
all-purpose flour	¼ cup (50 mL), unsifted
Parmesan cheese	¼ cup (50 mL), freshly grated
mild or medium Cheddar	2 cups (500 mL), grated
onion powder	½ tsp (2 mL)
soya sauce	¼ tsp (1 mL) or *to taste*
ginger	⅛ tsp (0.5 mL)
nutmeg	pinch
cooked chicken	2 cups (500 mL), diced
water chestnuts (optional)	1 x 10-oz (284-mL) can, washed, drained & sliced
extra-fine egg noodles	½ pkg (187 g)
cashews	½ cup (125 mL), chopped

Wash broccoli and cut into large flowerettes. Peel stems and slice thinly on the diagonal. Place broccoli in a 2-qt (2 L) saucepan with water and salt. Bring to a boil and simmer until tender-crisp. Drain broccoli, reserving broth, and refresh under cold water. Dissolve chicken bouillon cube in hot broth. Separate flowerettes from stems and set aside.

Sauce: Melt butter, add flour and cook for 2 minutes. Add reserved broccoli water, a third at a time, stirring continuously until sauce is smooth and thick. Add Parmesan, then Cheddar, a quarter at a time, stirring until melted. Stir in seasonings. Remove from heat and fold in chicken, water chestnuts and broccoli stems.

In a separate pot, cook egg noodles in boiling salted water for 5 minutes, or until tender, but firm. Drain, rinse under cold water, and drain again. Pour noodles into a buttered 9 x 13" (3.5 L) casserole. Arrange a broccoli border around casserole with flowerettes, and pour chicken mixture into the centre. Sprinkle with cashews, cover, and bake in a 375°F (190°C) oven for 30 minutes, or until heated through.

VARIATION

Substitute 1 x 170-g pkg. long grain and wild rice mix (available in chain stores) for egg noodles.

Turkey Casserole

Makes 4-6 servings

bread	8 slices, crusts removed
cooked turkey	3 cups (750 mL), diced
medium onion	1, chopped
celery	1 cup (250 mL), chopped
green pepper	½ cup (125 mL), chopped
medium or old Cheddar	1 cup (250 mL), grated
plain yogurt or mayonnaise	½ cup (125 mL)
salt & pepper	To taste
eggs	4, lightly beaten
milk	3 cups (750 mL)

Topping:

fresh garden tomatoes	3, thinly sliced
Cheddar	½-1 cup (125-250 mL), grated
paprika	

Grease bottom of 9 x 13" (3.5 L) casserole. Place 4 slices of bread on the bottom. In a large bowl, combine turkey, onion, celery, green pepper, Cheddar and mayonnaise or yogurt. Season with salt & pepper. Spread mixture on bread. Top with 4 slices of bread. In a smaller bowl, combine beaten eggs and milk. Pour over casserole. Cover casserole and refrigerate overnight. The next day layer sliced tomatoes over casserole and sprinkle with Cheddar, then paprika. Bake in a 325°F (160°C) oven for 1 hour. Let stand 10 minutes before serving.

VARIATION

Snow Crab Meat Casserole—Substitute 2 x 5-oz (2 x 142-g) cans of snow crab meat, drained, rinsed and flaked for turkey.
    Canned tuna or cooked chicken may also be substituted.

HINT

When garden tomatoes are not available, spread 1 x 10-oz (284 mL) can cream of mushroom soup (undiluted) on top of casserole, then sprinkle with Cheddar and paprika.

Individual Cheddar Meatloaves

Makes 4 servings

day-old bread	4 slices
milk	1 cup (250 mL)
medium or lean ground beef	1½ lbs (750 g)
ham or mortadella sausage	4 thin slices, cut into ½" (1.25 cm) squares
dry breadcrumbs	½ cup (125 mL)
eggs	2
Parmesan cheese	¼ cup (50 mL), freshly grated
mild or medium Cheddar	2 cups (500 mL), grated
salt	½ tsp (2 mL)
pepper	¼ tsp (1 mL)
nutmeg	⅛ tsp (0.5 mL)
all-purpose flour	¼ cup (50 mL), unsifted
olive or vegetable oil	2 Tbsp (25 mL)
butter	2 Tbsp (25 mL)
Port or Marsala wine	½ cup (125 mL)
water	½ cup (125 mL)
beef bouillon cube	1

Soak bread in milk for 10 minutes. Squeeze out moisture. In a large bowl combine meatloaf ingredients: ground beef, ham or sausage, bread-crumbs, eggs, cheese, soaked bread and seasonings. Mix well with hands and make 4 tight loaves. Roll loaves in flour to coat. In a Teflon-coated skillet, brown loaves on all sides in oil and butter. Transfer loaves to a heavy casserole with a lid, and place in a single layer. To oil and butter mixture add Port or Marsala. Cook until almost evaporated. Add water, and bring to a boil. Add bouillon cube and stir to dissolve. Pour liquid over loaves, cover casserole and bake in a 350°F (180°C) oven for 30 minutes. Remove loaves to a warmed platter. Thicken gravy if desired and serve with loaves.

HINT

Recipe may be halved. Make into one roll and simmer on top of stove (covered) for 30 minutes. Freshly sliced mushrooms may be added to gravy before placing in oven or simmering.

Chicken Rolls

Makes 4-6 servings

de-boned chicken breasts	6
thin slices cooked ham	3
mild or medium Cheddar	6 pieces, cut 1 x 2" (2.5 x 5 cm)
dry breadcrumbs	½ cup (125 mL)
sesame seeds	¼ cup (50 mL)
seasoned salt	1 tsp (5 mL)
dried dill weed	½ tsp (2 mL)
all-purpose flour	¼ cup (50 mL), unsifted
egg	1, lightly beaten
olive or vegetable oil	1 Tbsp (15 mL)
butter	1 Tbsp (15 mL)
white wine or dry vermouth	¼ cup (50 mL)
toothpicks	

Garnish: Fresh parsley & cherry tomatoes

Pound chicken fillets to ¼" (6 mm) thickness. On each piece, place ½ slice (approx. 2 x 3" or 5 x 7.5 cm) ham. Centre Cheddar pieces on top of ham. Tuck in sides and roll up each fillet tightly. Secure with toothpicks. Make breading: Combine breadcrumbs, sesame seeds, salt and dillweed. Coat chicken rolls in flour, dip in beaten egg, and roll all sides in breadcrumb mixture. Heat oil and butter in a Teflon-coated skillet. Fry rolls, covered, on medium heat for 15 minutes, turning to brown all sides. Remove toothpicks and place on warmed platter. Add wine or vermouth to skillet and stir over medium-high heat until almost evaporated. Pour over rolls. Garnish with parsley and cherry tomatoes and serve hot.

HINT

Rolls are also tasty cold. Take to outings along with potato salad.

Tuna Stuffed Peppers

Makes 8 servings

green pepper	8
tuna or olive oil	1 Tbsp (15 mL)
celery	½ cup (125 mL), chopped
onion	½ cup (125 mL), chopped
red bell pepper (optional)	½ cup (125 mL), chopped
seeded fresh tomato	½ cup (125 mL), chopped
black olives	⅓ cup (75 mL), chopped
fresh parsley	3 Tbsp (45 mL), finely chopped
capers	2 Tbsp (25 mL), drained & minced
fresh lemon juice	2 Tbsp (25 mL)
tuna	2 x 6½-oz (2 x 184-mL) cans, drained & flaked
mild or medium Cheddar	2 cups (500 mL), grated

Cut tops from peppers. Discard stems and mince tops. Remove seeds and membranes and blanch in boiling salted water for 5 minutes. Drain and refresh under cold running water. Invert on paper towels to drain. Make filling: in a skillet, heat oil and butter. Add minced pepper tops, celery, onion, red pepper and cook for 4 minutes. Add chopped tomato and cook 2 minutes. Transfer mixture to a medium bowl and add remaining ingredients. Stuff peppers and place in two buttered 8" (2 L) square baking dishes. Cover and bake in a 350°F (180°C) oven for 15-20 minutes or until heated through and Cheddar is melted. Serve hot or at room temperature.

Sole Au Fromage

Makes 3-4 servings

sole fillets	1 lb (500 g)
lemon	½, juiced
salt & pepper	To taste
real mayonnaise or plain yogurt	½ cup (125 mL)
Dijon-style mustard	1 tsp (5 mL)
mild or medium Cheddar	1 cup (250 mL), grated
paprika	To taste

Garnish: Lemon wedges, fresh parsley or baby dill

Sprinkle fillets with lemon juice, salt and pepper. Arrange in a single layer in a shallow, well-buttered baking dish. Cover fillets with a piece of waxed paper that has been buttered and place buttered side down. Bake in a 350°F (180°C) oven for 15 minutes or until fish may be easily flaked with a fork. Combine mayonnaise or yogurt with mustard. Spread on fillets. Sprinkle with Cheddar and paprika. Place under broiler until tops are lightly browned. Arrange on a heated platter. Garnish as desired.

VARIATION

Dill Sole au Fromage — Omit mustard and add 1 Tbsp (15 mL) snipped fresh baby dill to mayonnaise or yogurt.

Breaded Cheddar Sole — Bread sole fillets as in Cauliflower Cutlets. Sauté in equal parts melted butter and oil until fish is golden and crunchy. Haddock or cod may be substituted for sole.

Ham & Leek Pot Pie

Makes 4-6 servings

Filling:

leeks (approx. 8)	3 lbs (1.5 kg), white portion only
butter	¼ cup (50 mL)
pressed cottage cheese (Quark)	¾ cup (175 mL)
salt & pepper	To taste
ham	1 x 2-lb (1 kg) can, sliced ½" (1.25 cm) thick

Pastry:

frozen puff pastry	1 x 14-oz (398 g) pkg, thawed
medium or old Cheddar	1½ cups (375 mL), grated
Glaze:	egg yolk, beaten with 1 Tbsp (15 mL) milk

Filling: Cut leeks lengthwise, wash well and drain. Cut leeks into ½" (1.25 cm) slices. In a large skillet or saucepan, melt butter. Add leeks, cover tightly and cook over medium heat until softened. Remove from heat and stir in cottage cheese. Stir to combine well with leeks or until mixture is creamy. Add salt and pepper.

Lightly butter a deep 10" (1.5 L) baking dish. Arrange sliced ham on bottom of casserole and top with leek mixture.

Pastry: On a floured surface, roll puff pastry into a large rectangle. Sprinkle with Cheddar. Fold several times, and re-roll until Cheddar is incorporated into the dough. Fit dough over leek mixture, trim, and crimp border decoratively. Scraps of dough may be cut into shapes and applied to top with a little glaze. Brush top of pie with glaze and bake in a 400°F (200°C) oven for 30 minutes or until pastry is golden.

HINT

Cheddar Pastry (see Old-fashioned Apple Pie recipe), may be substituted for puff pastry.

For a very quick pastry, substitute one tube of crescent roll dough. Sprinkle 1½ cups (375 mL) Cheddar over leek mixture, before placing dough on top.

If pressed cottage cheese is not available, drain 1 cup (250 mL) cottage cheese in a sieve for several hours, and process until smooth with a blender or food processor.

Meat, Vegetable & Cheddar Chili

Makes 4-6 servings

medium or lean ground beef	1 lb (500 g)
oil	2 Tbsp (25 mL)
onion	2 cups (500 mL), sliced
celery	2 cups (500 mL), coarsely chopped
green pepper	2 cups (500 mL), coarsely chopped
fresh mushrooms	2 cups (500 mL) (halve if large)
tomato sauce	1 x 14-oz (398 mL) can
dried parsley	1½ tsp (7 mL)
chili powder	1½ tsp (7 mL)
dried oregano	1 tsp (5 mL)
salt	1 tsp (5 ml)
garlic powder	½ tsp (2 mL)
pepper	¼ tsp (1 mL)
medium or old Cheddar	1 cup (250 mL), grated

Topping:

medium or old Cheddar	1 cup (250 mL), grated

Pack ground beef into a rectangle and cut into 2" (5 cm) cubes. In a large Teflon-coated frying pan or electric frying pan, brown chunks in oil, stirring gently, so as not to crumble. Add onion, celery, green pepper, mushrooms, and sauté until tender-crisp. Add remaining ingredients and simmer uncovered for 20 minutes. Stir occasionally. Turn mixture into a 2-qt (2 L) casserole. Sprinkle with Cheddar Topping. Serve hot with a good crusty bread and salad.

HINT

This is even better when refrigerated overnight. Uncover casserole, and reheat in a 350°F (180°C) oven for 40-45 minutes. Sprinkle with Cheddar and serve. Excellent for a crowd, this recipe may be increased as required (however, cut back on seasonings and adjust to taste).

Eggplant Casserole

Makes 4-6 servings

eggplant	2 medium-large
bacon	5 slices, cut into 1" (2.5 cm) pieces
bacon fat	¼ cup (50 mL)
onion	1 medium, chopped
green pepper	2 small, chopped
garlic cloves	2, minced
bread	5 slices, crusts removed & cubed
black olives	½ cup (125 mL)
egg	1, lightly beaten
Cheddar	1 cup (250 mL), grated
pepper	½ tsp (2 mL)
salt, celery salt, & nutmeg	¼ tsp each (1 mL)

Topping:

Cheddar	1 cup (250 mL), grated

Peel eggplant, cube and cook in boiling salted water until tender (approx. 10 minutes). Drain in colander and squeeze out moisture with the back of a spoon (yields approx. 4 cups or 1 L eggplant). Fry bacon until crisp and drain. In bacon fat, sauté onion, green pepper and garlic until onion is golden. Pour mixture into a large bowl and add eggplant, bread cubes, bacon, olives, egg, Cheddar and seasonings. Combine mixture well and turn into buttered 2-qt (2 L) casserole. Sprinkle with Cheddar Topping and bake uncovered in a 350°F (180°C) oven for 30 minutes.

VARIATION

Eggplant and Clam Casserole—Add 1 x 10-oz (284 mL) can drained and rinsed baby clams to eggplant mixture.

HINT

This dish is attractive when baked in eggplant shells. Scoop out eggplant, sprinkle with salt and invert on paper towels to drain before filling.

Broccoli Mushroom Casserole

Makes 4-6 servings

long grain white rice	1 cup (250 mL), uncooked
celery	½ cup (125 mL), chopped
onion	½ cup (125 mL), chopped
cream of mushroom soup	1 x 10-oz (284 mL) can
water	½ cup (125 mL)
Cheddar	1 cup (250 mL), grated
mushrooms	1 lb (500 g)
broccoli	1 lb (500 g)

Topping:

Cheddar	1 cup (250 mL), grated

Rinse and drain rice. In a medium bowl, combine rice, celery, onion, mushroom soup and water. Turn into 9 x 13" (3.5 L) casserole. Sprinkle with Cheddar. Cover and bake in a 350°F (180°C) oven for 30 minutes. Meanwhile, wash mushrooms, and cut in half if large. Wash and cut broccoli into flowerettes. Peel stems and slice thinly on the diagonal. Stir mushrooms and broccoli into rice mixture. Layer flowerettes on top. Sprinkle with Cheddar Topping. Cover casserole and continue baking 30 minutes. Serve.

VARIATION

Substitute 1 x 170-g pkg. long grain & wild rice mix (available in chain stores) for all white rice.

Celery and Cabbage Bake

Makes 4-6 servings

cabbage	4 cups (1 L), coarsely chopped
celery	3 cups (750 mL), sliced
salt	1 tsp (5 mL)
caraway seeds	1 tsp (5 mL)
butter	2 Tbsp (25 mL)
all-purpose flour	¼ cup (50 mL), unsifted
milk	2 cups (500 mL)
beer	½ cup (125 mL)
old or extra-old Cheddar	1 cup (250 mL), grated
pepper	*To taste*

In a large pot, bring water to a boil. Add cabbage, celery, salt and caraway. Boil 5 minutes, then drain well in colander. Make sauce: Melt butter, add flour and cook, stirring 1 minute. Slowly add milk in a stream, stirring continuously until sauce is smooth and thick. Add beer and continue stirring until foam disappears. Cook until heated through. Add Cheddar, stirring until melted. Season sauce with salt and pepper to taste. Transfer vegetables to a buttered 2-qt (2 L) casserole and pour on sauce. Heat in a 350°F (180°C) oven for 30 minutes until hot.

VARIATION

Corned Beef or Ham Cabbage & Celery Bake—Add chunks of cooked ham or corned beef to vegetables before pouring on sauce.

HINT

For extra Cheddar flavour, top hot casserole with additional grated Cheddar, and broil briefly to brown lightly.

Cheese-Stuffed Zucchini Boats

Makes 6-8 servings (12 boats)

zucchini	6, approx. 7" (17.5 cm) long
eggs	2, lightly beaten
cottage cheese	½ cup (125 mL)
Cheddar	1½ cups (375 mL), grated
fresh parsley	2 Tbsp (25 mL), finely chopped
green onion	2 Tbsp (25 mL), finely chopped
salt	½ tsp (2 mL)
pepper	⅛ tsp (0.5 mL)
butter	2 Tbsp (25 mL)
dry breadcrumbs	¼ cup (50 mL)
raw sesame seeds	¼ cup (50 mL)

Boil or steam washed, whole, unpared zucchini for 10 minutes. Cut zucchini in half, scoop out seeds, sprinkle lightly with salt, and invert on paper towels to drain. In a medium bowl, combine eggs, cottage cheese, Cheddar, parsley, green onion, salt and pepper. In a small skillet, melt butter, and sauté breadcrumbs and sesame seeds until golden. Cool. Stuff zucchini boats with cheese filling and place in a single layer, in a shallow greased pan. Sprinkle with buttered crumb mixture. Bake in a 350°F (180°C) oven for 25-30 minutes.

HINT

May be prepared in advance and refrigerated until baking time. Allow an additional 10 minutes in the oven. Zucchini seeds are easily scooped out with a melon baller.

Broccoli & Mushrooms in Cheese Custard

Makes 4-6 servings

fresh broccoli	½ lb (250 g)
fresh mushrooms	½ lb (250 g)
eggs	4
milk	1 cup (250 mL)
salt	½ tsp (2 mL)
white pepper	¼ tsp (1 mL)
nutmeg	pinch
mild or medium Cheddar	1½ cups (375 mL), grated

Wash, trim and cut broccoli into flowerettes. Wash and slice mushrooms. Steam broccoli and mushrooms together for 10-15 minutes until broccoli is tender-crisp and mushrooms are cooked. Drain and cool. In a bowl, beat eggs with milk and seasonings. Arrange broccoli and mushrooms in a buttered baking dish. Sprinkle with Cheddar. Pour custard over vegetables. Set baking dish in a pan filled with 1" (2.5 cm) hot water. Bake in a 350°F (180°C) oven for 30-40 minutes, or until custard is set.

Endive and Leek Quiche

Makes 4-6 servings

Line a 10" (1 L) quiche pan with pastry. Prick bottom with fork and pre-bake in a 400°F (200°C) oven for 10 minutes.

Belgian endive	4 cups (1 L), chopped
leek	2 cups (500 mL), chopped
butter	¼ cup (50 mL)
sugar	½ tsp (2 mL)
salt	½ tsp (2 mL)
eggs	2
egg yolk	1
sour cream	1 cup (250 mL)
pepper	⅛ tsp (0.5 mL)
nutmeg	⅛ tsp (0.5 mL)
mild or medium Cheddar	1½ cups (375 mL), grated

Prepare endive and leek by halving lengthwise, washing well, and chopping coarsely. In a 2-qt (2 L) saucepan, melt butter and add endive, leek, sugar and salt. Cook covered, over moderate heat, for 10 minutes. Uncover and cook over high heat until liquid has evaporated. Cool mixture. In a bowl, combine remaining ingredients, beating lightly. Stir in vegetables. Pour into pre-cooked pastry shell and bake in a 350°F (180°C) oven for 40 minutes or until centre is set. Cool 10 minutes and serve.

VARIATION

Celery Leek Quiche—Substitute 4 cups (1 L) celery, sliced ¼" (6 mm) thin on the diagonal, for Belgian endive.

Avocado Tomato Pie

Makes 4-6 servings

Line a 10" (1 L) pie plate with Cheddar or plain pastry. Prick bottom with fork and pre-bake in a 400°F (200°C) oven for 15 minutes. Cool.

semi-soft avocados (just under ripe)	2
lemon	1, juiced
large fresh garden tomatoes	2, sliced ¼" (6 mm) thick
flour	2 Tbsp (25 mL)
dried sweet basil, garlic salt, salt and pepper	*To taste*
old Cheddar	1 cup (250 mL), grated

Peel, stone and slice avocados, and toss in lemon juice. Arrange half of the slices in a pinwheel pattern on baked crust. Arrange half of the slices of tomato, slightly overlapping, on top of avocado in pinwheel pattern. Sprinkle with half of the flour, and season lightly with sweet basil, garlic salt, salt and pepper. Sprinkle with half of grated Cheddar. Continue with a second layer of avocado. Top with remaining tomato, flour and seasonings. Sprinkle remaining Cheddar on top. Bake in a 400°F (200°C) oven for 30 minutes. Cool 10 minutes and cut in wedges.

NOTE

You may wish to salt and pepper avocado slices as well.

Spinach Cheddar Pie

Makes 4-6 servings

Line a 10" (1 L) pie plate with Cheddar or plain pastry. Prick bottom with fork and pre-bake at 400°F (200°C) for 10 minutes.

fresh spinach	2 x 10-oz (2 x 284 g) pkg or approx. 2 cups (500 mL) cooked
medium onion	1, chopped
butter	2 Tbsp (25 mL)
eggs	3, lightly beaten
creamed cottage cheese	1 cup (250 mL)
medium or old Cheddar	1 cup (250 mL), grated
nutmeg	pinch
salt & pepper	*To taste*

Cook spinach. Drain and squeeze out excess moisture. Chop and set aside. In a small skillet, sauté onion in butter until transparent. Cool. In a medium bowl, combine eggs, cottage cheese, chopped spinach, Cheddar, onion and seasonings. Pour into pre-baked pastry shell and bake in a 375°F (190°C) oven for 30 minutes or until set. Cool 10 minutes and cut into wedges.

HINT

For a tasty and quick pastry, use a tube of crescent roll dough. Line pie plate with triangles (points toward centre), join seams and pour in filling. (Pre-baking is not necessary).
Cooked frozen spinach may be substituted for fresh.

French Bread & Tomato Quiche

Makes 4-6 servings

French bread	4-5 slices
bacon	6 slices
bacon fat	6 Tbsp (90 mL)
onion	1 medium, chopped
green pepper	2 small, chopped
garlic cloves	2, crushed
sugar	2 tsp (10 mL)
salt	1 tsp (5 mL)
pepper	½ tsp (2 mL)
dried sweet basil	½ tsp (2 mL)
eggs	3, lightly beaten
fresh garden tomatoes	8 medium, thinly sliced
medium or old Cheddar	1 lb (500 g), thinly sliced, cut in 2 x 2" (5 x 5 cm) squares

Butter a 9 x 13" (3.5 L) pan or 12" (2 L) quiche pan. Toast French bread until lightly browned on both sides. Cut into 1" (2.5 cm) cubes and arrange on bottom of pan. Fry bacon until crisp, drain and crumble. Reserve 6 Tbsp (90 mL) bacon fat and in it sauté onion, green pepper and garlic until onion is golden. Stir in sugar and seasonings. Spread mixture over bread cubes. Then pour on beaten eggs. Sprinkle with bacon. Alternate tomato and cheese slices, overlapping in neat rows on top. Bake in a 350°F (180°C) oven for 25 minutes, until heated through. Broil top to brown if desired.

Cheddar Pizzas

Dough:

all-purpose flour	2 cups (500 mL), unsifted
baking powder	2 tsp (10 mL)
creamed cottage cheese	1 cup (250 mL)
milk	¼ cup (50 mL)
olive or vegetable oil	¼ cup (50 mL)
egg	1

In a large bowl, cut cottage cheese into flour and baking powder until mixture is crumbly. In a small bowl, beat milk, oil and egg lightly. Pour wet mixture into dry, all at once, and stir with fork to mix. Knead 1 minute to blend ingredients. Form into a ball. Roll out on floured surface. Fit dough into two 10" (25 cm) pizza pans or 1 large jelly roll pan. Spread with favourite Cheddar Toppings. Bake in a 400°F (200°C) oven for 30-35 minutes.

Toppings:
Ham & Pineapple with Cheddar — Drain and spread canned, crushed pineapple on bottom of crust. Sprinkle with chopped cooked ham. Sprinkle generously with Cheddar and bake.
Ham & Mushroom with Cheddar — Sprinkle a layer of chopped cooked ham on bottom of crust (or substitute Polish sausage or a variety of cold cuts). Sprinkle with a layer of Cheddar. Add a layer of chopped fresh mushrooms. Lightly sprinkle with Parmesan cheese. Top with a layer of grated Cheddar combined with Mozzarella, and bake.
Ground Beef Pizza — Spread bottom of crust with thick spaghetti meat sauce. Sprinkle generously with Cheddar and bake.
Bacon & Tomato with Cheddar — Sprinkle bottom of crust with crisp-cooked bacon. Add a layer of Cheddar. Add a layer of thinly sliced fresh tomatoes. Salt and pepper tomatoes, then lightly dust with flour. Sprinkle with more Cheddar and bake.
Mexican Pizza — Sauté ground beef, onion salt and pepper in a small amount of oil, until browned. Drain and crumble over bottom of crust. Sprinkle with chopped hot green chili peppers, combined with chopped pimientos. Sprinkle with Cheddar and bake.

Double-Crusted Cheddar Pizza Pies

Makes 2/8" (20 cm) pies (8-12 servings)

cottage cheese pizza dough (see Cheddar Pizzas)	1 Recipe
Polish sausage or smoked ham	2-4 cups (500-1000 mL), finely diced
mild or medium Cheddar	½ lb (250 g), thinly sliced
Mozzarella	½ lb (250 g), thinly sliced

Prepare cottage cheese dough and divide into 4 equal parts. Roll out 2 parts to fit the bottom and sides of two 8" (20 cm) round layer cake pans. Sprinkle equal amounts of sausage or ham on bottom crusts. Cover with equal amounts of Cheddar and Mozzarella. Roll out 2 top crusts and place atop pies. Press edges down to sides, and fold over to make a decorative roll. Cut two small steam vents on top. Place pies on centre rack and bake in a 400°F (200°C) oven for 35 minutes, or until crusts are browned. Cool 10 minutes before cutting into wedges.

HINT

Make several pies at one time, bake and freeze. Thaw and re-heat.

Cheddar Salmon Strudel

Makes 4 servings

Filling:

salmon	1 x 7.75-oz (220 mL) can, drained & flaked
mild or medium Cheddar	1 cup (250 mL), grated
onion	⅓ cup (75 mL), chopped
celery	⅓ cup (75 mL), chopped
green pepper	⅓ cup (75 mL), chopped
fresh baby dill	1½-2 Tbsp (20-25 mL), finely chopped
plain yogurt	3 Tbsp (45 mL)
seasoned salt	½ tsp (2 mL)
pepper	⅛ tsp (0.5 mL)
prepared tea biscuit mix	2 cups (500 mL)

Pastry:

old Cheddar	½ cup (125 mL), grated
milk	½ cup (125 mL)

Filling: In a medium bowl, combine salmon, Cheddar, onion, celery, green pepper, dill, yogurt, salt, and pepper.

Pastry: In a separate bowl, combine biscuit mix with old Cheddar. Stir in milk with a fork and knead mixture lightly 10 times. Roll dough on a floured surface into a 10 x 12" (25 x 30 cm) rectangle. Spread with filling and roll like a jelly roll. Place on a rimmed cookie pan, sealed side down. With a sharp knife, make 8-10 x 2" (5 cm) gashes on top of loaf. Turn loaf into horseshoe shape. Bake in a 375°F (190°C) oven for 30-35 minutes. Serve hot or cold with a salad or sliced garden tomatoes and cucumbers.

Cheddar Corn Fritters

Makes 2-4 servings

all-purpose flour	1 cup (250 mL), unsifted
baking powder	½ tsp (2 mL)
salt	½ tsp (2 mL)
Cheddar	1 cup (250 mL), grated
eggs	2, lightly beaten
canned corn kernels	1 cup (250 mL), drained
milk or beer	⅓-½ cup (75-125 mL)

In a medium bowl, blend flour with baking powder, salt and Cheddar. In a smaller bowl, mix eggs with corn and milk or beer. Pour corn mixture into flour mixture and stir until well combined (batter will be thick). In a large Teflon-coated skillet or an electric frying pan, heat ½" (1.25 cm) oil, until very hot. Drop fritter batter by large spoonfuls into hot fat, taking care that sides do not touch. Reduce temperature to low/medium, and fry fritters, covered, for 10-15 minutes or until puffy and golden on both sides. Serve hot with sweet preserves.

VARIATION

Add crumbled crisp bacon to the batter, or add clams or mussels.

SERVING SUGGESTION

Serve with bacon or sausages and maple syrup. Try with pineapple and ham slices.

Corn & Cheddar Croquettes

Makes 12-15 croquettes

potato	3 cups (750 mL), diced (approx. 2 large)
mild or medium Cheddar	1½ cups (375 mL), grated
corn kernels	1 x 12-oz (341 mL) can, drained
green onion	¼ cup (50 mL), finely chopped
green pepper	¼ cup (50 mL), finely chopped
salt	½-¾ tsp (2-3 mL)
pepper	¼ tsp (1 mL)
egg yolks	2
dry breadcrumbs	¾ cup (175 mL)

Breading:

dry breadcrumbs	2 cups (approx.) (500 mL)
egg whites	2, lightly beaten

In a large bowl place all ingredients except those for breading. Combine mixture well with hands and shape into 3" (7.5 cm) sausage shapes. Roll croquettes in egg white and then in breadcrumbs. Into a large Teflon-coated frying pan, pour ¼" (6 mm) depth of oil. When oil is hot, add croquettes to the pan (do not let croquettes touch). Reduce heat to medium and fry on all sides until well browned and crunchy.

VARIATIONS

Fish Patties — Substitute 1½ cups (375 mL) cooked and flaked salmon, tuna, cod or salt cod for corn kernels. Omit green pepper and substitute equal amount of freshly chopped parsley. Shape mixture into round patties and fry as directed above.

Corned Beef, Ham or Sausage Croquettes — Omit corn kernels and substitute 1½ cups (375 mL) finely cubed or flaked corned beef, ham or Polish kielbasa (sausage).

HINT

Make large batches of croquettes and freeze. Thaw and re-heat in a moderate oven.

Cauliflower Cutlets

Makes 4-6 servings

cauliflower	1, medium
dry breadcrumbs	1 cup (250 mL)
old Cheddar	1 cup (250 mL), grated
raw sesame seeds	½ cup (125 mL)
seasoned salt	1 tsp (5 mL)
eggs	2
milk	¼ cup (50 mL)

Garnish: Cherry tomatoes & fresh parsley

Trim outer leaves from cauliflower. Place whole cauliflower head in 1" (2.5 cm) water in a covered 3-qt (3 L) saucepan. Boil until tender-crisp. Refresh under cold water, drain and cool. Make breading: In a blender or food processor, process breadcrumbs, Cheddar, sesame seeds and salt together until very fine. Transfer to a pie plate. In a separate plate, beat eggs lightly with milk. Cut cauliflower into ½-¾" (1.25-1.8 cm) cutlets. Dip both sides of cutlet into egg mixture, then coat well with breadcrumb mixture. In a large Teflon-coated skillet or electric frying pan, melt equal parts of oil and butter to a ¼" (6 mm) depth. Sauté cutlets on medium heat until well browned and crisp on both sides. Transfer to a heated oval platter, layering so cutlets overlap slightly. Garnish with cherry tomatoes and fresh parsley and serve.

VARIATION

Kohlrabi Cutlets—Substitute cooked kohlrabi slices for cauliflower. Peel kohlrabi, boil whole until tender, then cool and slice.

HINT

This dish may be prepared in advance and re-heated in a 350°F (180°C) oven for 20-25 minutes. Or, bread cauliflower and refrigerate until just before frying.

SERVING SUGGESTION

Also delicious served with a Cheddar Cheese Sauce (serve sauce separately).

Fried Rice & Cheddar

Makes 4 servings

bacon	4 slices
onion	1 cup (250 mL), chopped
fresh parsley	½ cup (125 mL), finely chopped
white or brown cooked long-grain rice	2½-3 cups (625-750 mL)
soya sauce	1 tsp (5 mL)
salt	½ tsp (2 mL)
pepper	⅛ tsp (0.5 mL)
Cheddar	1 cup (250 mL), grated
Garnish: Hard-cooked eggs	halved lengthwise & quartered
crisp bacon (as prepared below)	4 slices

In a Teflon-coated skillet, fry bacon until crisp. Drain and crumble. Set aside, reserving fat. In bacon fat, sauté onion until transparent. Add parsley, rice, soya sauce, salt and pepper. Stir-fry over medium heat until lightly browned. Add Cheddar and heat while tossing lightly to coat Cheddar. Mound mixture on a heated platter. Garnish with a border of eggs sprinkled with bacon.

VARIATION

A number of other vegetables may be added and sautéed before adding rice, (e.g sliced celery, broccoli buds, water chestnuts etc).
Fried Barley & Cheddar —Substitute cooked pearl or pot barley for rice.

Cheddar Home Fries

Makes 4-6 servings

sunflower seed oil	2 Tbsp (25 mL)
large onion	1, chopped
medium potatoes	6, peeled & cubed
seasoned salt	*To taste*
medium or old Cheddar	2 cups (500 mL), grated

In a large Teflon-coated skillet or electric frying pan, heat oil to medium temperature (350°F or 180°C). Add onion and potatoes and steam/fry covered, turning occasionally with a spatula. When almost tender, sprinkle with seasoned salt to taste. Remove lid. Add Cheddar and turn potatoes several times until browned and crunchy.

Sweet Cheddar

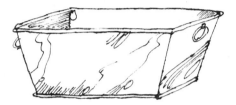

Cheddar Bread

Makes 2 loaves

cold water	1¾ cups (425 mL)
salt	2 tsp (10 mL)
cornmeal	½ cup (125 mL)
maple syrup or liquid honey	½ cup (125 mL)
lukewarm water	½ cup (125 mL)
sugar	1 tsp (5 mL)
active dry yeast granules	2½ tsp or 1 pkg (12 mL)
all-purpose flour	5 cups (1.25 L), unsifted
medium or old Cheddar	¾ lb (350 g), cut into ¼" (6 mm) cubes

In a 1-qt (1 L) saucepan, mix cold water, salt and cornmeal. Stirring continuously, bring to a boil, and cook for 1 minute until thickened. Remove from heat and stir in maple syrup or honey. Cool mixture to lukewarm. Meanwhile, in a large bowl sprinkle yeast over warm water and sugar. Let stand 10 minutes, then stir in cooled cornmeal mixture. Stir in 3 cups (750 mL) of flour. Turn dough onto floured surface and knead remaining 2 cups (500 mL) of flour into dough. Transfer to a well-buttered bowl and turn dough to cover with butter.

Cover bowl with a dampened cloth and let rise in a warm place until double in bulk (approx. 1½ hours). Punch down dough. Turn onto surface sprinkled with cornmeal. Knead in Cheddar pieces, a little at a time. Grease two 8" (20 cm) round cake pans. Divide dough in half and shape into two round loaves. Place in pans and let rise until double in bulk (approx. 1 hour). Bake bread in a 350°F (180°C) oven for 30-40 minutes or until crusty and browned, top and bottom.

HINT

This bread is even better the next day, toasted and spread with strawberry preserves or honey. Freezes well.

Cheddar Pull-Apart Rolls

Makes 18-24 large rolls

warm water	¼ cup (50 mL)
sugar	½ tsp (2 mL)
active dry yeast granules	2½ tsp or 1 pkg (12 mL)
milk	¾ cup (175 mL), scalded
butter	½ cup (125 mL), chopped into pieces
sugar	¼ cup (50 mL)
eggs	3, lightly beaten
all-purpose flour	4½-5 cups (1125-1250 mL), unsifted
mild or medium Cheddar	3 cups (750 mL), coarsely grated

In a small bowl, sprinkle yeast over warm water combined with ½ tsp
(2 mL) sugar. In a large bowl, combine scalded milk, butter and ¼ cup
(50 mL) sugar. Stir mixture until butter has melted. Cool to lukewarm.
Stir in yeast mixture and eggs. Add 3 cups (750 mL) flour all at once. Turn
dough onto floured surface and knead in remaining flour, until dough is
smooth and elastic (approx. 10 minutes). Form dough into a ball, and
turn in a well-buttered bowl, to coat ball with butter. Cover with a
dampened cloth and let rise in a warm place until double in bulk (approx.
1 hour).

Butter a 10" (2.5 L) tube pan. Punch down dough. On a floured
surface, roll dough into a 12 x 16" (30 x 40 cm), ¼" (6 mm) thick, rectangle. Sprinkle dough evenly with Cheddar, and roll like a jelly roll. Cut
into ½" (1.25 cm) slices. Place slices, cut side down, in tube pan. Repeat to
make three layers. Let rise in a warm place until almost double in bulk
(approx. 1 hour). Bake bread in a 375°F (190°C) oven for 35 minutes until
golden. (Bread should sound hollow when tapped on bottom). Turn out
on cooling rack for 10 minutes. Pull apart at the table and serve with
butter.

Cheddar Tea Biscuits

Makes 16-18

all-purpose flour	1 cup (250 mL), unsifted
graham flour	1 cup (250 mL), unsifted
baking powder	1 Tbsp (15 mL)
baking soda	½ tsp (2 mL)
salt	½ tsp (2 mL)
butter	¼ cup (50 mL), chilled
old Cheddar	½ cup (125 mL), grated
plain yogurt	¾ cup (175 mL)
egg	1
light molasses	1 Tbsp (15 mL)

In a medium bowl, stir together dry ingredients. Cut butter into mixture with a pastry blender. Stir in Cheddar. In a separate bowl, beat together yogurt, egg and molasses. Add to flour mixture all at once, stirring to combine. Turn dough onto floured surface and knead 30 seconds. Roll dough to ½" (1.25 cm) thickness. Cut into 2½" (6.25 cm) rounds with a cookie cutter. Place on ungreased baking sheet. If desired, brush tops with a little milk and sprinkle with additional Cheddar. Bake in a 425°F (220°C) oven for 15 minutes.

Cream Scones

Makes 8 scones

all-purpose flour	2¼ cups (550 mL), unsifted
sugar	3 Tbsp (45 mL)
baking powder	1 Tbsp (15 mL)
salt	½ tsp (2 mL)
butter	¼ cup (50 mL), chilled
old Cheddar	½ cup (125 mL), grated
eggs	2
10% or 18% cream	½ cup (125 mL)

In a medium bowl, stir together dry ingredients. Cut butter into mixture with a pastry blender. Stir in Cheddar. In a separate bowl, beat eggs with cream. Add to flour mixture all at once and stir to combine. Turn dough onto floured surface and knead 30 seconds. Pat dough into a 10" (25 cm) round. Place on ungreased cookie sheet and cut into 8 equal wedges. Brush lightly with extra cream and sprinkle with additional Cheddar. Bake in a 450°F (230°C) oven for 15 minutes, until golden brown on top. Cut scones in half and serve warm, with unsalted butter and sweet preserves.

SERVING SUGGESTION

Traditionally served with Devonshire cream and crushed berries. If unavailable, serve with heavy cream, whipped.

Graham Nut Loaf

Makes 2 Loaves

butter or margarine	1 cup (250 mL), softened
sugar	1 cup (250 mL)
medium or old Cheddar	1 cup (250 mL), finely grated
eggs	5
pure vanilla extract	1 tsp (5 mL)
graham flour	1 cup (250 mL), unsifted
cake & pastry flour	1½ cups (375 mL), unsifted
walnuts or pecans	1 cup (250 mL), coarsely chopped

Butter and flour two 5 x 9" (1.5 L) loaf pans. In the bowl of an electric mixer, cream butter or margarine with sugar until fluffy. Add Cheddar and combine well. Add eggs, one at a time, beating well after each addition. Stir in vanilla. On low speed of mixer, add graham flour, mixing until well incorporated. Add cake & pastry flour, a quarter at a time, mixing well after each addition. Stir in nuts. Spread batter in prepared loaf pans. Bake in 350°F (180°C) oven for 50-60 minutes, or until cake tester inserted in centre comes out clean. Let loaves cool for 10 minutes and remove from pans. Serve thinly sliced with butter.

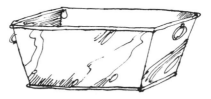

Cheddar Nut Muffins

Makes 10 Muffins

cake & pastry flour	1½ cups (375 mL), unsifted
baking powder	1½ tsp (7 mL)
baking soda	½ tsp (2 mL)
salt	½ tsp (2 mL)
old Cheddar	½ cup (125 mL), grated
egg	1
sunflower seed oil	¼ cup (50 mL)
maple syrup	½ cup (125 mL)
milk	1 cup (250 mL)
pure vanilla extract	1 tsp (5 mL)
pecans or walnuts	1 cup (250 mL), finely chopped

In a medium bowl, combine well flour, baking powder, soda, salt and Cheddar. In a smaller bowl, combine well egg, oil, maple syrup, milk and vanilla. Combine wet and dry mixtures together with nuts, and fold together until just mixed. Spoon into greased muffin pan. Bake in a 375°F (190°C) oven for 15-20 minutes. Remove from pan and cool on rack.

Cheddar Shortbread

Makes approx. 3 dozen

butter	½ cup (125 mL), softened
icing sugar	¼ cup (50 mL)
cornstarch	1 Tbsp (15 mL)
all-purpose flour	1 cup (250 mL), unsifted
mild or medium Cheddar	1 cup (250 mL), grated
lemon or orange rind	½ tsp (2 mL), finely grated

Place all ingredients in a medium bowl. Mix well with hands to form a smooth, soft dough (knead approx. 5 minutes). Roll dough into cylinders with waxed paper and refrigerate overnight. The next day, remove cylinders from refrigerator ½ hour before baking. Slice dough ⅓" (8 mm) thick and place on ungreased cookie sheet. Bake in a 300°F (150°C) oven for approx. 15 minutes.

Cranberry Cheddar Cookies

Makes approx. 3 dozen

butter	½ cup (125 mL), softened
granulated sugar	1 cup (250 mL)
egg	1
fresh orange juice	¼ cup (50 mL)
all-purpose flour	2½ cups (625 mL), unsifted
baking powder	1 tsp (5 mL)
baking soda	½ tsp (2 mL)
salt	½ tsp (2 mL)
medium or old Cheddar	1 cup (250 mL), grated
fresh or frozen cranberries	2 cups (500 mL), chopped

Glaze:

icing sugar	1 cup (250 mL), sifted
fresh orange juice	2 Tbsp (approx.) (25 mL)

In a large bowl, cream butter with sugar. Add egg and orange juice. In a separate bowl, combine flour, baking powder, soda, salt and Cheddar. Add flour mixture to creamed mixture together with cranberries. Stir well to blend. Drop batter from teaspoonsfuls on ungreased cookie sheet, placing 1" (2.5 cm) apart. Bake in a 375°F (190°C) oven for 18-20 minutes. Make a thin glaze of icing sugar and orange juice. Brush on cooled cookies.

HINT

To chop cranberries more easily, place in food processor together with ¼ cup (50 mL) sugar and process until chopped. (Calculate sugar into recipe).
If cookies are left unglazed, you may wish to adjust granulated sugar to 1¼ cups (300 mL).

Oatmeal Cheddar Crispies

Makes 35-2 x 2" (5 x 5 cm) squares

butter	½ cup (125 mL)
maple flavouring	½ tsp (2 mL)
uncooked rolled oats	2½ cups (625 mL)
brown sugar	¾ cup (175 mL), lightly packed
old Cheddar	½ cup (125 mL), grated
baking powder	½ tsp (2 mL)
salt	¼ tsp (1 mL)

In a small skillet, melt butter. Cool and stir in maple flavouring. In a large bowl, mix remaining ingredients. Pour melted butter over crumbs and rub mixture together with hands until well moistened. Press mixture into a greased 11 x 7" (27.5 x 17.5 cm) rimmed cookie pan. Even surface by pressing down with back of fork. Bake in 400°F (200°C) oven for 10 minutes. While warm, cut into 2 x 2" (5 x 5 cm) squares with a sharp knife. When fully cooled, remove squares from pan (pieces will be crisp) and snap apart.

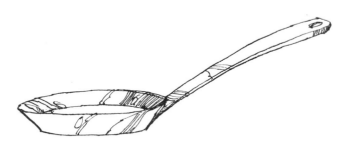

Cheddar Peanut Butter Cookies

Makes 2-2½ dozen cookies

smooth or crunchy peanut butter	1 cup (250 mL)
brown sugar	½ cup (125 mL), lightly packed
granulated sugar	½ cup (125 mL)
mild or medium Cheddar	1 cup (250 mL), finely grated
egg	1
pure vanilla extract	1 tsp (5 mL)

In a medium bowl, mix all ingredients with a spatula or wooden spoon until well combined. Roll into 1" (2.5 cm) balls and place on ungreased cookie sheet. Flatten with a fork dipped in flour. Bake in a 325°F (160°C) oven for 15-18 minutes. Cool 2 minutes on cookie sheet before removing from pan.

VARIATION

Cheddar Peanut Crispies—Stir 2 cups (500 mL) Rice Krispies cereal into dough. Drop by teaspoonfuls onto ungreased cookie sheet. Flatten slightly and bake in a 325°F (160°C) oven for 18 minutes. Makes 3 dozen.

Raspberry Cheddar Squares

Makes approx. 36

butter	¼ cup (50 mL)
sugar	¼ cup (50 mL)
mild or medium Cheddar	1 cup (250 mL), grated
all-purpose flour	1½ cups (375 mL), unsifted
baking powder	1½ tsp (7 mL)
raspberry jam	

In a medium bowl, combine all ingredients except jam with hands. Press ¾ of the mixture on bottom of a buttered 8" (2 L) square pan. Spread with raspberry jam. Crumble remaining Cheddar mixture on top. Bake in a 350°F (180°C) oven for 20-25 minutes (until browned on top). Cool and cut into small squares.

HINT

Substitute strawberry or apricot jam, or crabapple or apple jelly, for raspberry jam.

Cheddar Pumpkin Pie

Makes 1 large pie or 2 small

Line a 10" (25 cm) pie plate or two-8" (20 cm) pie plates with plain or Cheddar pastry (see Old-fashioned Apple Cheddar Pie). Refrigerate shells while preparing filling.

eggs	3
sugar	¾ cup (175 mL)
mild or medium Cheddar	1 cup (250 mL), finely grated
canned pumpkin	1½ cups (375 mL)
cinnamon	½ tsp (2 mL)
ginger	½ tsp (2 mL)
nutmeg	¼ tsp (1 mL)
salt	¼ tsp (1 mL)
evaporated milk	1 cup (250 mL), undiluted

In the bowl of an electric mixer, beat eggs with sugar and Cheddar until well combined and Cheddar pieces are barely visible. Add pumpkin, spices and salt, and beat 1 minute more. Add milk. Pour mixture into pastry shell(s). Form a foil collar over rim of crust to prevent crust from burning (remove collar after 30 minutes in oven). Bake pie in a 450°F (230°C) oven for 10 minutes. Reduce temperature to 350°F (180°C) and bake 50 minutes longer for one large pie, 40 minutes for two smaller pies. Pies are done when centre is set and stainless steel knife inserted in centre comes out clean. Remove pie(s) to cooling rack and serve warm or cold with whipped cream.

HINT

2 unthawed frozen pie shells may be substituted.

Cranapple Cheddar Squares

Makes 15-4 x 4" (10 x 10 cm) squares

Line a large jelly roll pan with plain or Cheddar Pastry (see Old-fashioned Apple Cheddar Pie). Cover pastry bottom with waxed paper and weigh down with dried beans. Pre-bake in a 400°F (200°C) oven for 10 minutes. Remove paper and beans.

Filling:

fresh or frozen cranberries	3 cups (750 mL)
medium apples	8, pared, cored & sliced
granulated sugar	1 cup (250 mL)
cornstarch	¼ cup (50 mL)
salt	½ tsp (2 mL)

Topping:

butter	1 cup (250 mL), softened
brown sugar	1 cup (250 mL), lightly packed
all-purpose flour	1 cup (250 mL), unsifted
uncooked rolled oats	3 cups (750 mL)
old Cheddar	1½ cups (375 mL), grated

Filling: In a 4-qt (4 L)saucepan, combine cranberries, apples, granulated sugar, cornstarch and salt. Cook covered, over medium heat, stirring often, until cranberries pop (approx. 10 minutes).

Topping: In a medium bowl, rub together butter, brown sugar, flour, oats and Cheddar. Spread filling on pre-baked pastry. Crumble oatmeal/ Cheddar mixture over top. Bake in a 375°F (190°C) oven for 30-35 minutes. Allow 10 minutes to cool before cutting into 4 x 4" (10 x 10 cm) squares. Serve warm or cold with whipped cream or ice cream.

VARIATION

Cranapple Cheddar Crisp—Omit crust. Turn filling into a buttered 9 x 13" (3.5 L) baking pan. Top with oatmeal/Cheddar mixture. Bake in a 375°F (190°C) oven for 30-35 minutes. Serve warm or cold.

NOTE

The filling is tart. You may wish to increase granulated sugar to 1½ cups (375 mL). Taste before adjusting.

Apple Cheddar Crumble

Makes 4-6 servings

all-purpose flour	1 cup (250 mL), unsifted
salt	½ tsp (2 mL)
brown sugar	¼-½ cup (50-125 mL), lightly packed
mild or medium Cheddar	1 cup (250 mL), grated
butter	¼ cup (50 mL), softened
apples	5 cups (4 large) (1.25 L), cored, peeled and sliced
allspice	⅛ tsp (0.5 mL)
Amaretto liqueur	2 Tbsp (25 mL)
brown sugar	½ cup (125 mL), lightly packed

In a medium bowl, stir together dry ingredients, including Cheddar. Rub in butter to make a crumble. In a separate bowl, toss apple slices with allspice, liqueur and brown sugar. Spread in a buttered 8" (2 L) square pan. Distribute crumble mixture evenly on top. Bake in a 350°F (180°C) oven for 40 minutes or until apples are cooked and crumble is golden brown. Serve warm or cold with thick cream.

HINT

Rum or brandy may be substituted for Amaretto. Or mix ½ tsp (2 mL) almond flavouring with 2 Tbsp (25 mL) water.

Apricot Bread Pudding

Makes 6-8 servings

pre-sliced white or brown bread	12 slices, crusts removed
softened butter	
apricot jam	½ cup (125 mL)
mild Cheddar	1 cup (250 mL), grated
eggs	2
evaporated milk	½ cup (125 mL), undiluted
whole or 2% milk	½ cup (125 mL)
maple syrup	¼ cup (50 mL)
pure vanilla extract	1 tsp (5 mL)

Lightly butter both sides of bread. Place 4 slices on bottom of buttered 8" (2 L) square baking pan. Spread with ¼ cup (50 mL) jam. Sprinkle with ½ cup (125 mL) Cheddar. Place 4 slices of bread on top. Spread with remaining jam and sprinkle with Cheddar. Place remaining slices on top. Beat eggs with milks, syrup and vanilla. Pour mixture evenly over bread. Bake in a 350°F (180°C) oven for 45 minutes. Serve warm with whipped cream.

VARIATION

Strawberry or raspberry jam may be substituted for apricot jam.

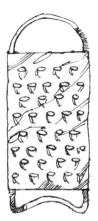

Old-Fashioned Apple Cheddar Pie

Makes 2 large pies

Pastry:

all-purpose flour	6 cups (1.5 L), unsifted
sugar	1 tsp (5 mL)
salt	1 tsp (5 mL)
pure lard	1 lb (500 g), chilled
old Cheddar	1 cup (250 mL), grated
ice water	15 Tbsp (225 mL)

In a large bowl, combine flour, sugar and salt. Cut lard into flour with pastry blender until mixture resembles coarse meal. Stir in Cheddar. Sprinkle ice water over mixture all at once, and combine quickly with fork. Form into a large ball and divide into 4 equal portions. Wrap each portion in waxed paper and refrigerate until needed.

Filling:

cooking apples, peeled, cored & sliced	14 cups (3.5 L)
granulated or brown sugar, lightly packed	$\frac{2}{3}$ cup (150 mL)
cornstarch	2 Tbsp (25 mL)
salt, ginger & cinnamon	$\frac{1}{2}$ tsp each (2 mL)

Roll out 2 portions of pastry to line two-10" (25 cm) deep-dish pie pans. Make filling. Toss sliced apples with remaining ingredients. Divide filling between two pies. Roll out remaining 2 portions of pastry to make top crusts. Trim, seal edges and pinch decoratively. Make two small slashes on tops. Bake in a 400°F (200°C) oven for 1 hour. Remove pies to cooling rack. Serve warm or cold with whipped cream or a slice of sharp Cheddar on top.

HINT

Bake one pie and freeze the second unbaked.

Apple Cheddar Dumplings

Makes 6 large dumplings

frozen puff pastry	1 x 14 oz (398 mL) pkg
brown sugar	⅓ cup (75 mL), lightly packed
walnuts or pecans	⅓ cup (75 mL), chopped
raisins or chopped dates	⅓ cup (75 mL)
butter	3 Tbsp (45 mL), softened
large apples	6, peeled & cored
old Cheddar	1½ cups (375 mL), grated

Glaze: egg yolk, beaten with 1 Tbsp (15 mL) milk

Thaw frozen puff pastry at room temperature for 1 hour. Make filling: with fingers, rub together sugar, nuts, raisins or dates and butter. Stuff cored apples with filling. Prepare pastry; on a floured surface, roll out puff pastry into a large rectangle. Sprinkle with Cheddar. Fold pastry over several times. Re-roll and fold several times, incorporating Cheddar into the pastry. Roll pastry into a 12 x 18" (30 x 45 cm) rectangle. Cut into 6 x 6" (15 x 15 cm) squares. Place 1 stuffed apple on each square. Bring opposite corners together and pinch seams together. Place dumplings seam side down and at least 2" (5 cm) apart in a baking pan (or two 9 x 13", 3.5 L pans). With left-over scraps of pastry, cut attractive leaf shapes, and apply to tops of dumplings with egg glaze, then brush dumplings with glaze. Bake in a 400°F (200°C) oven for 40 minutes, or until apples are cooked. (Test apples with a long cake tester.) Serve dumplings warm with whipped cream.

VARIATION

Peach Cheddar Dumplings—Substitute 6 large fresh peaches, halved and stoned, for apples. Stuff peach halves with filling, and press two halves together.

HINT

Prepare ahead and refrigerate until baking time.

Apple Cheddar Cheesecake

Makes 8 servings

Shortbread Crust:

butter or margarine	½ cup (125 mL), softened
granulated sugar	¼ cup (50 mL)
pure vanilla extract	½ tsp (2 mL)
all-purpose flour	1 cup (250 mL), unsifted

Filling:

cream cheese	8 oz (250-g pkg), softened
granulated sugar	¼-⅓ cup (50-75 mL)
mild or medium Cheddar	1 cup (250 mL), finely grated
eggs	2
pure vanilla extract	½ tsp (2 mL)
all-purpose flour	1 Tbsp (15 mL)

Topping:

brown sugar	¼ cup (50 mL), lightly packed
all-purpose flour	1 Tbsp (15 mL)
ground ginger	¼ tsp (1 mL)
apples	4 cups (1 L), peeled and sliced
walnuts or pecans	¼ cup (50 mL), chopped

Crust: In a small mixing bowl, beat butter with sugar until light and fluffy. Add vanilla. Work flour into mixture until a ball of dough forms. Place dough between two sheets of waxed paper and roll into 10" (25 cm) circle. Remove paper and turn pastry into 9" (23 cm) springform pan. Gently press dough against sides and bottom of pan. Refrigerate 30 minutes.

Filling: In the small bowl of an electric mixer or food processor, beat cream cheese, sugar and Cheddar until well blended (Cheddar bits should not be visible). Add eggs, vanilla and flour. Beat until smooth. Pour filling into chilled crust.

Topping: In a large bowl, combine sugar, flour and ginger. Toss with apples. Arrange apple slices on top of filling. Sprinkle with nuts.

   Bake in a 450°F (230°C) oven for 10-12 minutes. Reduce temperature to 375°F (190°C) and bake 30 minutes longer, or until apples are tender. Cool 5 minutes before loosening cake from rim. Cool and serve with whipped cream.

Creamy Cheddar Cheesecake

Makes 8-12 servings

Graham Nut Crust:

graham wafer crumbs	1 cup (250 mL)
brown sugar	¼ cup (50 mL), lightly packed
walnuts or pecans	¼ cup (50 mL), finely chopped
butter or margarine	¼ cup (50 mL), melted

Filling:

cream cheese	8 oz (250-g pkg), softened
mild Cheddar	2 cups (500 mL), finely grated
plain yogurt	2 cups (500 mL), drained 4-8 hours
granulated sugar	¾ cup (175 mL)
eggs	3
egg yolks	2
nutmeg	⅛ tsp (0.5 mL)
lemon or orange rind	½ tsp (2 mL), grated

Crust: In a medium bowl, combine crumbs, sugar and nuts. Add butter and mix well. Press onto bottom of 9" (23 cm) springform pan. Bake in a 325°F (160°C) oven for 10 minutes. Remove to cooling rack.

Filling: In a small bowl of electric mixer or food processor, beat cream cheese with Cheddar until well blended (Cheddar bits should not be visible). Add yogurt and sugar. Beat until smooth, scraping sides of bowl occasionally. Add eggs, yolks, and flavourings. Blend well. Pour filling into cooled crust. Bake in a 475°F (240°C) oven for 12 minutes. Reduce temperature to 250°F (130°C) and bake 1½ hours longer. Remove to cooling rack. Carefully loosen cake from rim of pan and cool completely. Serve chilled with fresh berries.

VARIATION

Instead of Graham Nut Crust, make Shortbread Crust (see Apple Cheddar Cheesecake). Work in ½ cup (125 mL) finely chopped nuts with flour. Turn pastry into pan and prick bottom crust with fork. Pre-bake in a 400°F (200°C) oven for 10 minutes. Cool on wire rack before filling.

For a firmer, European-style cheesecake texture, add 2 Tbsp (25 mL) all-purpose flour to filling in food processor bowl. Drained canned sour cherries may be spread over pre-baked crust before pouring on filling.

Apple Rings in Batter

Makes 2-3 servings

apples	2-3, peeled, cored & sliced ¼" (6 mm) thick
egg	1
sugar	2 Tbsp (25 mL)
salt (optional)	½ tsp (2 mL)
milk	1 cup (250 mL)
all-purpose flour	1 cup (250 mL), unsifted
old Cheddar	½ cup (125 mL), grated

Prepare apples. In a medium bowl, beat egg with sugar and salt. Add milk and flour alternately. Stir in Cheddar. Set temperature in an electric frying pan to 375°F (190°C) and in it, heat ½" (1.25 cm) oil. (Teflon-coated skillet may also be used). Dip apple rings in batter, coating well on both sides. Fry in oil, turning once, until golden on both sides. To prevent batter from absorbing fat, take care not to prick apples. Drain, and serve hot with maple syrup, jam or cinnamon sugar.

VARIATION

Substitute drained pineapple rings for apple rings.

HINT

When in a hurry, add 1½-2 cups (375-500 mL) chopped apple to batter to make one large Apple Cheddar Pancake. Serve hot in wedges. These reheat very well in a moderate oven or microwave. Also good cold for bag lunches.

Noodle Pudding

Makes 4-6 servings

fine egg noodles	½ pkg (187 g)
eggs	4, lightly beaten
sugar	⅔ cup (150 mL)
creamed cottage cheese	1 cup (250 mL)
mild or medium Cheddar	1 cup (250 mL), grated
milk	1½ cups (375 mL)
nutmeg	⅛ tsp (0.5 mL)
raisins, chopped dates or apricots	½ cup (125 mL)
butter	2 Tbsp (25 mL)

Cook egg noodles in boiling salted water for 5 minutes. Drain in colander, rinse and drain again. In a large bowl, combine beaten eggs, sugar, cottage cheese, Cheddar, milk, nutmeg and dried fruit. Fold in egg noodles. Pour mixture into buttered 9 x 13" (3.5 L) baking pan. Dot top of casserole with butter. Bake in a 350°F (180°C) oven for 45-50 minutes. Serve warm.

HINT

For an even richer flavour, cut 4 oz or 125 g cream cheese into ½" (1.25 cm) cubes, and add to egg mixture just before folding in noodles.

SERVING SUGGESTION

A very nutritious lunch choice for children. Make ahead and reheat in microwave or moderate oven. Also good cold in a lunch bag.

Index